W9-BAO-043

Concorde

ZENITH PRESS

FRÉDÉRIC BENIADA - MICHEL FRAILE

Contents

The decision to take Concorde out of service was a hard one, but it was the right choice at the right moment. Concorde will always remain part of British Airways and occupy a special place in the hearts of passengers and staff throughout the world.

ROD EDDINGTON, CHIEF EXECUTIVE OF BRITISH AIRWAYS

GOD SAVE CONCORDE

October 24, 2003: 15.50. The last-ever British Airways Concorde flight from New York touches down at London Heathrow. Five minutes later, a second Concorde arrives from Edinburgh, then a third from the Bay of Biscay off the French coast.

Before landing, all three staged a fly-past over London, nose lowered, landing gear down. Behind the gates of Buckingham Palace, the royal household poured out into the courtyard to witness this unique event. Secretaries, workmen, footmen, kitchen staff and butlers—differences in status forgotten, all united by the desire to bid farewell to Concorde. "It was a beautiful sight; it just made you want to cry," wrote one reporter present.

In France, a few months earlier, there had been no official ceremony to mark Concorde's passing, for fear of reopening the wounds caused by the accident at Gonesse which claimed 113 lives. But on Saturday May 31, 2003, at 17.45, thousands of members of the public gathered at Roissy-Charles-de-Gaulle airport to see Air France Flight 001 land for the final time. Massive queues formed on the roads beneath the approach path as drivers abandoned their vehicles. Eyes fixed on the sky, they paid their silent tribute.

"Concorde to be retired." After twenty-seven years of good and loyal service. The rumor had been growing ever since the tragedy of July 25, 2000. In fact, despite the numerous technical modifications made subsequently and a brief return to service on November 7, 2001, Concorde never really recovered from the trauma surrounding her only accident. The Iraq conflict, the economic situation and the aftermath of 9/11 finally persuaded both British Airways and Air France to cease investment. Since the outbreak of hostilities in the Persian Gulf, passenger numbers had plummeted below the 25 per cent threshold, while maintenance costs had soared by nearly 70 per cent. "It was a decision we didn't take lightly," explained an emotional Jean-Cyril Spinetta, President of Air-France, during a press conference. "But we had no choice. The whole operation was losing money badly. Under the circumstances, it was becoming unreasonable to carry on."

Concorde's detractors justify her withdrawal on the grounds that the aircraft was too old and too costly, an anachronism with out-of-date components and awesome fuel consumption. Admittedly, she was thirsty, needing three times as much fuel as a conventional design. The oil crises of 1973 and 1979 had brought this home, giving Concorde her first real battering. More seriously, perhaps, she had a major design flaw: her dimensions were conceived for transatlantic flights, making her unsuitable for longer hauls, as the need for frequent refueling stops tended to nullify her advantage in terms of flying time and speed. In addition, the reluctance of the Americans to allow her to land at most US airports because of environmental concerns virtually limited her role to that of a prototype. Only the major east coast airports (at New York and Washington) were of any real practical use to Concorde since an inland airport involved overflying land, which at supersonic speeds was not legal in the USA.

Only sixteen aircraft were ever built and in twenty-seven years of commercial exploitation, only some four million passengers traveled on Concorde—the world's Boeing 747 fleet would carry the same number in a few weeks. And even if, at the end of the 1990s, British Airways and Air France succeeded in breaking even—investment costs excluded—they never achieved sustained profitability. One thing, however, is certain: the demise of Concorde sounded the death-knell of a unique aircraft. She was recognized by everyone and praised all over the globe both for the elegance of her lines and the technological skills represented by her development in the early 1960s.

"Be careful!" Daedalus warned his son Icarus in the Greek myth. "Keep midway between the sun and the waves. If you fly too low, the sea will drag down your wings; too high, and the sun will burn them. Fly between the two. Ignore Bootes and the Great Bear, and the naked sword of Orion. Be sure to follow me."
(Ovid, *Metamorphoses*.)

Neither too low nor too high; not too far to the north or the south. Daedalus' admonitions to his son were those of caution and prudence; weren't they the first two men to don wings and fly? Daedalus knew from experience that Man's genius is not without pitfalls and that it can lead him to acts of the utmost folly. Once upon a time, had he not killed his own nephew and pupil, Perdix, because he had surpassed his master, inventing the saw and the compass? He had flung the young man from the top of the Acropolis; as he fell, he was transformed into a partridge. It was not without apprehension, then, that Daedalus, "like a mother bird teaching her tender offspring to fly," watched as his son learned to work the first wings in human history.

Today, the tale of Icarus is often portrayed as the myth that inspired our love-affair with aeronautics and space travel: the conquest of the skies by Man, now on equal footing with the birds, even the gods. But the legend also sounds a note of warning: a fall as precipitous and deadly as that of Icarus awaits those who allow themselves to be carried away by hubris, the arrogance of the creative genius. "Icarus flies too near the sun, and its fierce heat softens the scented wax holding his feathers. As it melts, he finds himself waving only his bare arms. Now he cannot cleave the skies and the air no longer buoys him up; his lips still cry his father's name as the deep-blue waves engulf him." (*Ibid.*)

Yet disobedience is not necessarily synonymous with arrogance, nor is prudence a characteristic of youth! Those who see the Icarus legend as a warning against human pride are probably right; but perhaps we should also see it as a simple, commonsense encouragement to discretion and moderation. Who, re-reading Ovid, is Icarus, if not a child whose father has just presented him with the most extraordinary of all toys?

Our beautiful bird also scorched her wings on that fateful day in July 2000; so badly that three years later she folded them for ever. She sprang from the imagination of a new race of Daedaluses, the twentieth-century engineers passionate to escape their own labyrinths —the limitations of the sound barrier and the demands of the boom in commercial aviation. In pursuit of their aims they adopted the same motto as the sportsmen who, at the dawn of the same century, had also rediscovered the road to Olympus: "Faster, higher, stronger". On board their bird in her white livery they took on the wildest of challenges, accumulated the most astonishing records. Some had the honor of piloting her, others were proud merely to serve.

But, cynics will argue, wasn't it all for nothing in the end? So many resources, so much money squandered, so much talk and build-up, only for the beautiful bird to end up in a museum! Will the Minoses of the twenty-first century have the last word? Did our engineers and policy-makers sin through excess of pride?

We can and should defend the beautiful white bird in terms of technological advances, European co-operation and international competition, but it is not enough. Child of these modern day Daedaluses, Concorde was first and foremost the heir of Icarus, the boy who discovered a then-nameless joy—flight. Will we, in our turn, be worthy of such a heritage?

Dr Jacques Arnould, Project Leader, CNES [French Space Agency], January 2005.

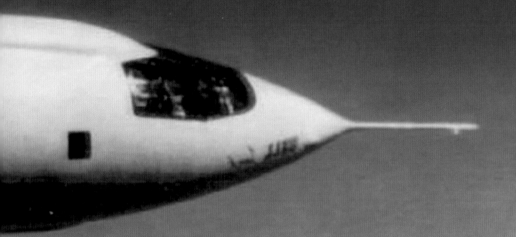

THE SUPERSONIC
ADVENTURE

> *I couldn't believe my eyes! I was flying faster than sound!*
> *It was as smooth as a baby's bottom...* CHUCK YEAGER, 1947

BREAKING THE SOUND BARRIER

The idea of an aircraft flying faster than sound was aired for the first time in 1935 in Rome. In a room in the Villa della Farnesina, fifty or so engineers and aerodynamics experts from all over the world gathered for a conference on high-speed flight. Among them was a certain Adolf Buseman, a shy thirty-four-year-old engineer from Dresden, Germany. His presentation bristled with technicalities such as supersonic speeds, delta wings and the relationship between peak efficiency and Mach number. By the end of the Second World War, jet propulsion was leaving the technology of the propeller further and further behind. On November 7, 1945, the British captured the first world record for a jet aircraft when Group Capt. H.J. Wilson reached a speed of 606.397 mph (975.875 kph) in a Gloster Meteor IV. In France, a handful of manufacturers—Marcel Bloch (later Dassault), a survivor of the death camps, René Leduc and Lucien Servanty—resumed the experiments they had begun during the Roaring Twenties. The first French jet, built by a team from the Société nationale de constructions aéronautiques du Sud-Ouest (SNCASO), was the SO 6 000 Triton.

It was designed in secret by Lucien Servanty and developed on the initiative of Marcel Riffard, an engineer working on high-speed aircraft for Caudron. The SO 6 000 Triton took to the skies for the first time on November 11, 1946. At the controls was Daniel Rastel, SNCASO's chief test pilot. With this success, France became the sixth country to master jet flight, after Germany (Heinkel), Italy (Caproni), Great Britain (Gloster), the United States (Bell) and the Soviet Union (Mig 9).

Meanwhile, the Americans took the lead. On October 14, 1947, at the controls of his Bell X-1, Chuck Yeager broke the fateful sound barrier for a period of some twenty seconds. A resounding sonic boom announced his entry into the history books. It had been done at last—and this was only the beginning. At Edwards Air Force Base, California, record after record was to fall. At the start of the 1950s, the Douglas D-558-2 Skyrocket, developed by the National Advisory Committee for Aeronautics (the future NASA), underwent its test flights. With its small wings and almost perfect aerodynamics, it reached Mach 1.88 (1,237 mph/ 1,990 kph) in August 1951, and Mach 2 in November 1953. Not one to be left behind,

Chuck Yeager pushed back the limits even further; in December of the same year he flew his X1-A at Mach 2.44. "I couldn't believe my eyes! I was flying faster than sound! It was as smooth as a baby's bottom. Grandma could have been up there sipping lemonade!" commented Yeager after breaking the sound barrier in October 1947.

THE SHAPE OF THINGS TO COME: THE ESPADON GRIFFON AND THE MIRAGE III

At the end of the war, French designers displayed enormous ingenuity as they attempted to recover dominant positions in the national market. After the Triton, SNCASO launched the SO 6 020 Espadon. But this fighter was always underpowered, despite the adaptation of the Rolls-Royce Nene engine, the most powerful jet available under license at the time. Eventually, on December 15, 1953, the aircraft attained Mach 1 in level flight. Despite these setbacks, the engineers, among them Lucien Servanty, did not lose heart. SNCASO's R & D department then came up with the SO 9 000 Trident. This had straight wings equipped with two 400 kg (882 lbs) Turbomeca Marboré II wing-tip jets, plus three SEPR rockets each producing 9,920 lbs of thrust. The Trident's

performance looked promising. Unfortunately, the second prototype was lost on its first flight. Re-engined in 1956 with Viper jets, the SO 9 050 Trident climbed to over 49,000 ft (15,000 m) and maintained Mach 1.55 in level flight. In opposition to SNCASO, three other constructors flung themselves into the contest to fly ever faster. The Société nationale des constructions du Sud-Est (SNCASE) produced the SE Durandal, a delta-winged supersonic design, while Dassault was working on its Mirage III. At the same time Arsenal, SFECMAS, and Nord Gerfaut were developing respectively the ARS 2301, the ARS 1301 and then the Gerfaut 1402, the first design to exceed Mach 1 in horizontal flight (August 1954). Some time later, Gerfaut and SFECMAS were absorbed by a new company, the Société des constructions aéronautiques du Nord, which brought out the Nord 1 500 Griffon I— first flight September 1955—and eventually the Griffon II. From the start, this aircraft boasted a combination engine (ramjet plus conventional turbojet); on February 25, 1959, it beat the world record for a closed 62-mile (100-km) circuit at a speed of 1,018 mph (1,638 kph) and, on October 13, 1959, touched Mach 2.2. It was flown by André Turcat, Concorde's future test pilot.

PAGES 16,17
On October 14, 1947, a Bell X-1 (originally the XS-1) broke the sound barrier at 42,000 ft (12,800 m). The aircraft was powered by a rocket-motor burning liquid oxygen and a mixture of alcohol and water. Unable to take off under its own power, the Bell X-1

was launched in flight from the bomb bay of a Boeing B-29. Chuck Yeager, then a young captain of 24, became the fastest man in the world. On the ground, a huge sonic boom, the first in aviation history, marked Yeager's entry into the history books.

OPPOSITE
The Bell X-1 was affectionately baptized *Glamorous Glennis* by Chuck Yeager in tribute to his wife. With the help of Yeager, America grabbed one record after another.

The Bell X-1 was succeeded by the Bell X-2 which, in August 1956, reached an altitude of 125,853 ft (38,360 m). A month later, it passed Mach 3.

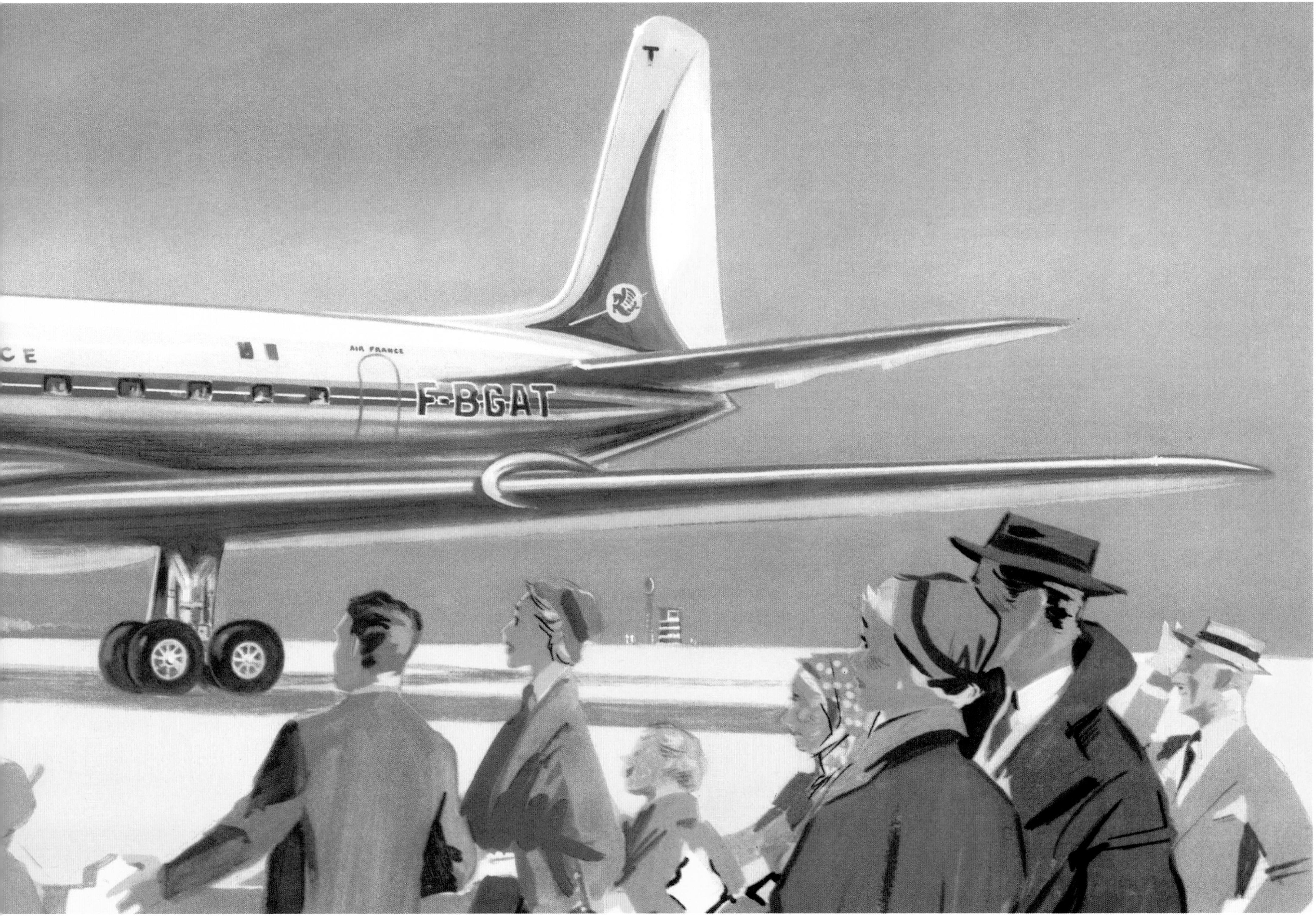
CE
AIR FRANCE
F-BGAT
T

> *All the calculations show it can't work.*
> *There's only one thing to do:* make *it work.*

PIERRE GEORGES LATÉCOÈRE (1883–1943, AVIATION ENTREPRENEUR)

RENÉ LEDUC AND THE RAMJET

The origin of the ramjet goes back to the early days of aviation with articles published by René Lorin in the periodical *Aérophile*. Lorin described the principle of the ramjet, with no propeller or moving parts. But without a flying test bed fast enough to start a ramjet, he was unable to test his invention. It consequently fell into oblivion. The idea of the ramjet was only revived in 1933 by René Leduc, who was working for the aircraft firm of Louis Breguet on advanced methods of propulsion. Leduc obtained a patent for his "thermopropulsive tube" (as he called his ramjet). The military soon became interested in the project, and the first contracts for trials were signed with the French Air Force in 1934. During the 1938 Paris Air Show, a mock-up of the aircraft, the Leduc 010, was displayed to the public with claims as futuristic as its design: 620 mph (1,000 kph) at around 100,000 ft (30,000 m)! But then came the war and René Leduc's projects were put on the back-burner. In 1945 the engineer resumed his work in even greater earnest, the 1937 agreement having been resurrected. His brief was the construction of two prototypes and their mountings, to be installed on the four-engined He 274 and Languedoc. The combustion system consisted of five concentric rings equipped with three circular burner units. The aircraft was constructed entirely around the ramjet. The first successful flight of a ramjet aircraft took place on April 21, 1949. The performance of the Leduc 010 was impressive. Its maximum climb rate exceeded 65 ft/sec (20 m/sec) at around 30,000 ft (10,000 m), twice that of the contemporary F-86. The following year, these trials led to an improved prototype. The Leduc 016 differed from its predecessor by the presence, at the wing tips, of two Turbomeca Marboré jet engines with a thrust of 2,865 lbs. The two 016 prototypes would serve as test beds for the development of the 021 and then of the final version: the 022 S (S for Supersonic). This aircraft resembled something from a science-fiction movie. It was distinguishable from the somewhat pot-bellied 010 and the 016 by its striking cylindrical fuselage aft of a streamlined cockpit encased in a huge expanse of transparent Plexiglass. An Atar 101D 3 turbojet incorporated into the rear of the fuselage and producing 6,170 lbs of thrust provided auxiliary power allowing the fighter to take off and land under its own power. The ramjet, over 6 ft (2 m) in diameter, employed a more sophisticated combustion system than earlier models, with six stacked concentric combustion chambers.

The Leduc 022 made its maiden flight on December 26, 1956. But it proved too thirsty—it could stay airborne for just five to thirty minutes depending on flying conditions, altitude and speed. It could climb easily at Mach 0.95, but could not break the sound barrier. Its combustion system was very hard to regulate, functioning poorly at high altitudes, and the wings generated greater drag than initially anticipated. Towards the end of 1957, a fire damaged the 022 prototype. At the time, public expenditure was under severe budgetary restraint, and in January 1958 the government abandoned the program. The cancellation marked the end of Leduc's participation in ramjet experiments. Yet his technological achievement was not entirely lost to the world; Dassault made use of its hydraulic relay system for the servocontrols of the Mirage, and the idea of the ramjet was given new life by the Société de constructions aéronautiques du Nord when they built the Griffon. The Nord 1 500 Griffon was far and away a better airplane.

THE VICTOR, VALIANT AND VULCAN

After the Second World War, the British went to great lengths to build a major strategic air force. This was based on the entry into service, between 1955 and 1958, of three designs: the Handley Page Victor, the Vickers Valiant and the Avro Vulcan, the latter being the world's largest delta-wing bomber. It was not long before it assumed the key role in Britain's airborne nuclear deterrent, as well as serving as a test bed for Bristol-Siddeley's Olympus engines.

The civil aircraft industry was not slow to profit from advances made by the military. As far back as 1942, Winston Churchill had asked the Brabazon Committee to investigate the viability of a long-haul passenger aircraft. De Havilland engaged on a project they called the DH106 Comet. The aircraft was powered by four De Havilland "Ghost" DGT-3 engines producing 5,068 lbs of thrust enabling it to reach a cruising speed of nearly 500 mph (800 kph) at around 39,000 ft (12,000 m). This was a record for a commercial aircraft. The Comet's inaugural flight took place in July 1949: it was certified in January 1952 and entered service with BOAC four months later on the London–Johannesberg route. Henri Ziegler, chief executive of Air France, was carried away with enthusiasm and put in orders for his company. Then came disaster. On January 10, 1954, Comet G-ALYP ("Yoke Peter") exploded in mid-flight a few minutes after taking off from Rome's Ciampino airport. The crew had no time to transmit an SOS. Three months later, in April 1954, Comet G-ALYY ("Yoke-Yoke") suffered the

PAGES 20, 21
The Comet entered commercial service on the London–Johannesberg route in May 1952. De Havilland executives were over the moon: "We conquered the waves under Elizabeth I; under Elizabeth II we'll rule the air." But dreams for the Comet's future swiftly turned into a nightmare.

On January 10 and April 8, 1954, less than two years after the inauguration of the first commercial company to employ jet-powered airliners, two Comets broke up in mid-flight. Experts concluded that both aircraft had suffered explosive depressurization resulting from metal fatigue.

same fate over the Bay of Naples. Investigations were carried out by experts from the Royal Aircraft Establishment at Farnborough; they concluded that the aircraft had suffered explosive depressurization as a result of metal fatigue. In 1958 a new version of the Comet was brought into service. But the industry had lost confidence in the design and when De Havilland published its data following the crashes, both Boeing and Douglas were able to benefit from their research. Nevertheless, the Comet 4 was the aircraft used by BOAC when they started the first transatlantic jet passenger airline service in 1958, just beating Boeing to it, but the Comet was never taken on in great numbers.

THE JETLINER COMES OF AGE

On October 27, 1958, a new chapter in the history of air transport opened at Le Bourget with the arrival of Flight 114: Pan Am B707-120 "Jet Clipper America". The prefect of Paris was there to welcome the 111 passengers and 11 crew of the first Boeing 707 to make a commercial crossing between New York and Paris. Juan Trippe, Pan Am's president, had personally bid bon voyage to the four-engined jetliner as it departed Idlewild (now JFK) Airport on October 26 at 19.30, bound for Gander, Newfoundland, where it had to refuel before crossing the Atlantic—at the time, the

runway at Idlewild was too short to allow a 707 to take off with a full load of fuel. Once above the Atlantic, the aircraft flew at around 31,000 ft (9,500 m) at speeds touching 620 mph (1,000 kph). Boeing had triumphed. All the same, the Seattle firm was not the first to fly a commercial jetliner over the North Atlantic. Only three weeks before a Comet 4 had inaugurated a weekly link between London Heathrow and Idlewild. The day of the jetliner had arrived. It remained to be seen whether it would prove profitable on short- and medium-haul journeys.

In 1951, Air France submitted to the domestic aircraft industry a plan for a 36–40 tonne airplane capable of flying fully laden between Paris and London or Casablanca. Four maunfacturers lined up to compete: Breguet, Hurel-Dubois, Sud-Ouest and Sud-Est Aviation. In Toulouse, Pierre Satre entrusted Project X210 to a team led by Pierre Escola. Sud-Est Aviation's plan was an audacious one. The engines would no longer be mounted in classic fashion beneath the wings, but on the fuselage. Such an arrangement offered numerous advantages. It eliminated the unpleasantness and danger of sound vibrations produced by the engines; with engines under the wings, vibrations would normally strike the fuselage at the level of the pressurized cabin.

Additionally, the new positioning of the engines would mean that the thrust line would pass almost exactly through the aircraft's centre of gravity, increasing its stability, even if an engine failed. Nor had the French failed to learn from the tragic fate of the Comet. Pierre-Paul Valat, a structural engineer and specialist in materials resistance, contacted De Havilland immediately the London public inquiry declared the Comet "unfit to fly". He concluded an agreement with the British engine manufacturer allowing him to study the effects of structural fatigue on aircraft subject to pressure variations during high-altitude flight.

THE CARAVELLE

The Caravelle incorporated the Comet's nose design. Prototype 01 took to the air on May 27, 1955. Some months later, Air France announced its intention of ordering twelve with an option on another dozen. French president General de Gaulle traveled to Toulouse on board the twin-engine jet on February 14, 1959; in March, Air France and SAS jointly inaugurated the first commercial flights. Hoping for permission to operate within the USA, Sud Aviation entered into negotiations with Douglas for sub-contracting the aircraft. Discussions dragged on as Douglas deliberately extracted all the information they could about the airplane and

began developing their own Project 2086, the DC-9, a close copy of the Caravelle. The main difference between the two was that the DC-9 had a "T-tail" (horizontal stabilizer atop the fin) and was to enjoy a commercial success denied the Caravelle. "The Americans rubbished the Caravelle," lamented Beranard Lathière, future chief executive of Airbus Industrie. "They claimed it was outmoded, dangerous, practically ready for the scrapheap." In the end, 282 Caravelles were sold. Though no more than a break-even venture, it did enable Airbus Industrie to avoid a number of possible pitfalls in future projects. Additionally, the Caravelle served as a basis for somewhat more unconventional projects. On March 30, 1960, Marcel Dassault and Georges Héreil decided to combine their experience with the Caravelle and the Mirage III and IV to produce a 75-tonne aircraft flying at Mach 2.2 and with a range of over 2,000 miles (3,500 km). The project came to nothing. But in 1966, during a press conference, Marcel Dessault was to explain: "I proposed fitting a Mirage IV with a pressurized fuselage seating twelve passengers. Obviously, flying twelve passengers from Paris to Rome or Berlin was not economic with a Mirage IV, but it would allow us to get to grips with the basics of a supersonic aircraft."

The Caravelle, the world's first medium-haul twin-jet passenger aircraft, took to the skies on May 27, 1955. Its success encouraged engineers to take up the challenge of supersonic flight. This was a revolutionary design. The jet engines were mounted not under the wings but in nacelles either side of the fuselage, near the tail. The result was an aircraft that was less noisy for the passengers, more aerodynamic, and safer. The absence of vibrations—the gold standard of comfort—was illustrated with a coin balanced on edge on a passenger table. On March 24, 1959, Air France took delivery of its first two models, christened respectively *Alsace* and *Lorraine*. A few weeks afterwards, the Caravelle made its inaugural flight over Istanbul, capital of Turkey. On board were the president of Air France, Max Hymans, members of the French parliament, press barons and industrialists. The Caravelle was the pride of Air France. General de Gaulle employed it on his official visits. "Swift, sure and gentle Caravelle," was the French president's verdict after a trip to Toulouse in February 1959.

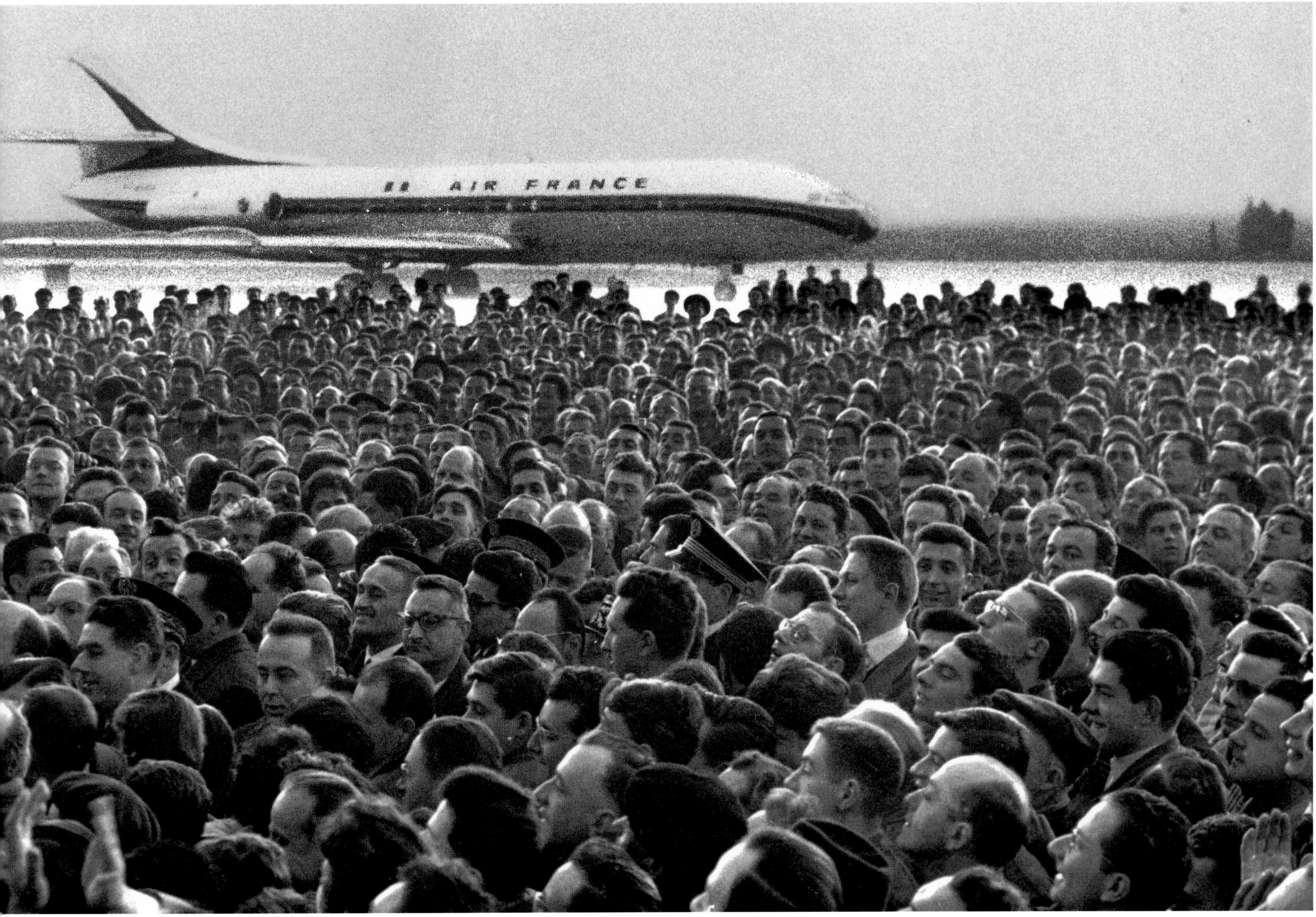
AIR FRANCE

OPPOSITE
One of the most memorable features of the Caravelle was its distinctive teardrop-shaped windows, another "first" for Sud-Aviation. These made it easier for passengers to enjoy the views of the sky.
LEFT
Orly Airport. The aircraft nearest the camera is a Boeing 707, with two Caravelles in the background.

FROM THE MIRAGE IV TO CONCORDE

On March 30, 1960, Marcel Dassault and Georges Héreil, head of Sud Aviation, signed a co-operation agreement. The two firms intended to pool their experiences with the Caravelle and the Mirage III and IV. The result was a number of projects for an SST or supersonic transport aircraft. "Dassault had been interested in a supersonic airliner since 1959. Our company envisaged using two Mirage IV prototypes for test purposes. In 1960, Louis Bonte, Chief Aeronautical Engineer at the government agency Direction Technique et Industrielle, said to my father and Georges Héreil, boss of Sud Aviation: 'Dassault specializes in supersonic aircraft, Sud Aviation in transport. So come up with a plan for a supersonic transport aircraft.' From that moment, the R & D departments of both companies exchanged a mass of information, with Dassault providing polar curves and aerodynamic data relating to the structure and the delta wing, etc., which they had amassed from experience with the two Mirage versions. Things moved up a gear with the arrival on the scene of the British Aircraft Corporation. Dassault now had a representative on the Anglo-French steering committee composed of major manufacturers.

Dassault continued to supply Sud Aviation with all its know-how on delta-winged aircraft, with particular regard to structural problems, as well as test-flight reports on the Mirage IV, which were vital for developing the new prototype. At the same time, the government placed the Mirage IVA No. 4 at state-owned Sud Aviation's disposal so that André Turcat could familiarize himself with a deltawing airplane. In the plans for the construction of prototypes, British interests limited the participation of Dassault to providing the outer wing sections for a total of nine aircraft. Nowadays, Dassault Aviation continues to work on supersonic civilian flight; we have invested in a prospective study for a supersonic Falcon through the international project known as HISAC [High Speed Aircraft]."

Serge Dassault, President of Groupe Dassault, February 2005.

OPPOSITE
Dassault's design for a supersonic airliner was inspired by the Mirage IV. The aircraft destined to fly at Mach 2.2 and with a range of 2,175 miles (3,500 km) was of similar design, including the wings and two semicircular air intakes supplying each of the two jets.

AVION PRE-SERIE

DETAIL FABRICATION
MANUFACTURE BREAKDOWN

10	POINTE AVANT	FUSELAGE NOSE	**BAC** Weybridge
11	FUSELAGE AVANT	FORWARD FUSELAGE	**BAC** Filton
12	FUSELAGE INTERMEDIAIRE	INTERMEDIATE FUSELAGE	**SUD** Marignane
13	ONGLETS AV VOILURE	FORWARD WING	**SUD** Bouguenais
14	PARTIE CENTRALE	CENTRE WING	**SUD** Marignane
15	" " 41 à 46	" "	**SUD** "
16	" " 46 à 54	" "	**SUD** Bougenais
18	" " 54 à 60	" "	**SUD** Toulouse
20	" " 60 à 66	" "	**SUD** "
	" " 66 à 72	" "	**SUD** St Nazaire
21	VOILURE EXTREME	OUTER WING	**GAM** Dassault
23	ELEVONS	ELEVONS	**RHOR**
24	FUSELAGE ARRIERE	REAR FUSELAGE	**BAC** Preston
25	NACELLES	NACELLES	**BAC** Filton & Rhor
	TUYERES	NOZZLE	**SNECMA**
26	DERIVE	FIN	**BAC** Weybridge
27	GOUVERNAIL	RUDDER	**BAC**
51	TRAIN PRINCIPAL	LANDING GEAR MAIN	**HISPANO SUIZA**
	TRAIN AVANT	LANDING GEAR NOSE	**MESSIER**

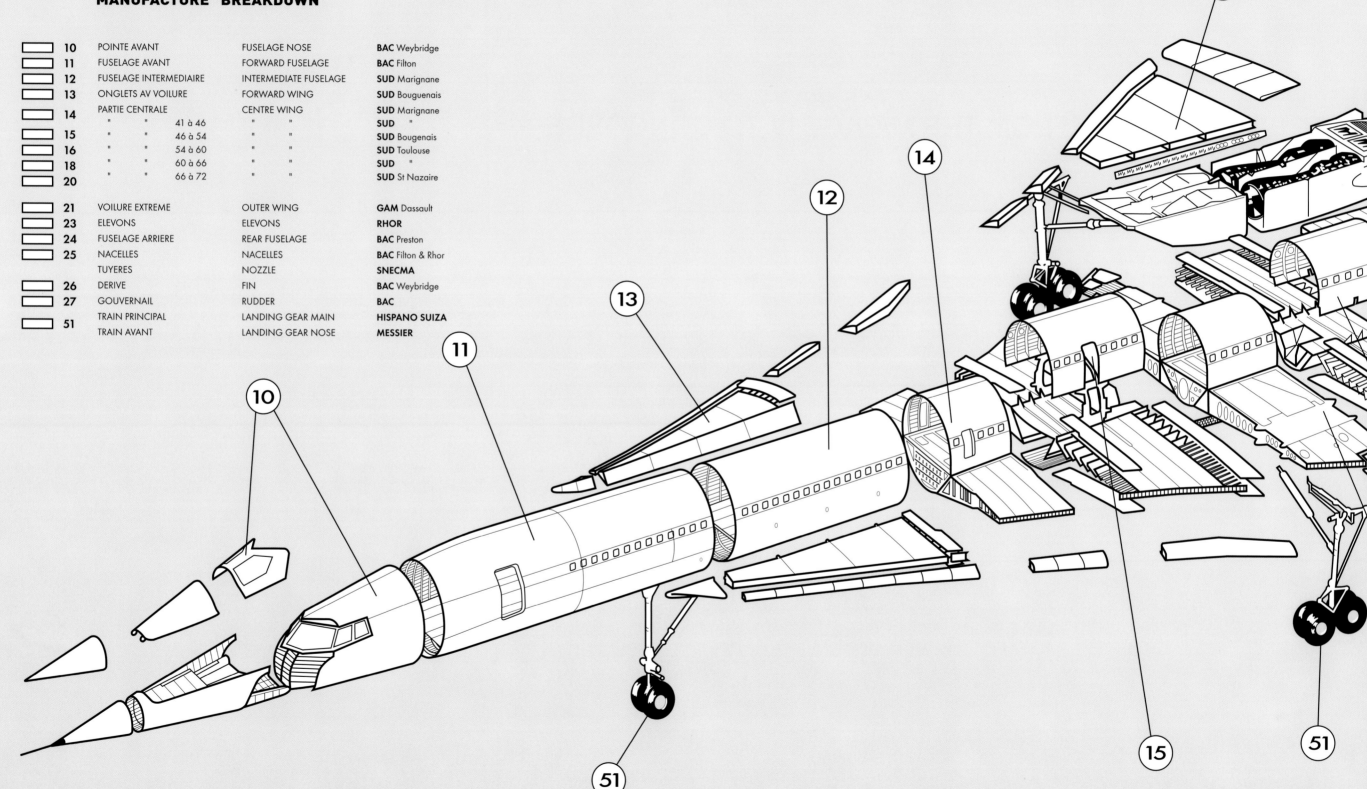

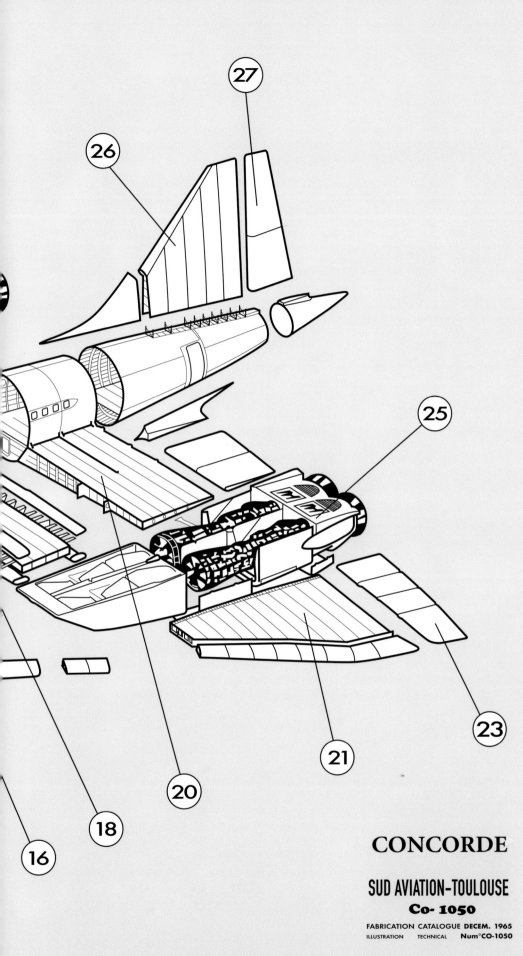

DESIGN AND CONSTRUCTION

CONCORDE

SUD AVIATION-TOULOUSE
Co- 1050

FABRICATION CATALOGUE DECEM. 1965
ILLUSTRATION   TECHNICAL   Num°CO-1050

THE SUPERSONIC JETLINER

It was not until 1961 that the first serious discussions took place between the British and French on plans for a supersonic passenger aircraft. A year later, on November 29, 1962, Geoffroy Chodron de Courcel, the French Ambassador in London, and Julian Amery, British Minister of Aviation, signed the agreement that irrevocably committed both governments to all stages of development including mass-production of the final design. The two nations decided to share on an equal basis the total costs of research and development. The airplane would be constructed by Sud Aviation and BAC; it would be equipped with British Olympus 593 engines developed from the earlier versions of the Olympus, already in service on the Avro-Vulcan since 1953. These engines were to be improved and brought up to date by the French company SNECMA and the British firm of Bristol-Siddeley (absorbed into Rolls-Royce from 1966). With the aim of ensuring strict equality in the division of labor between Paris and London, the agreement of November 29, 1962, provided for the establishment of steering committees under alternate chairmanship. The arrangement, however, was extremely rigid and cumbersome; the committees consisted of dozens of officials from both countries, a situation that slowed down progress considerably. Paradoxically, the construction of a supersonic transport aircraft (SST) appeared to increase the differences between France and Britain and their governments, rather than bringing them closer. Next, a name was needed for the new aircraft. The idea that was eventually accepted came from the 18-year-old son of BAC's Head of Sales and was proposed to the French. In a speech on January 13, 1963, General de Gaulle duly baptized the prototype *Concord* [*sic*], celebrating the "new *entente cordiale*." Ironically, he then proceeded to slam the door on Britain's entry to the Common Market. From this point on, administration of the project was in the hands of a project leader jointly appointed by the French and British cabinets, assisted by civil servants to ensure that things kept on course. In 1964, however, the Conservative government in Britain was succeeded by a Labour administration which pledged to withdraw from the project for both economic and political reasons. The French threatened London with legal action. In a dramatic gesture, General de Gaulle banged his fist on the table and exclaimed: "Concorde will be built, with or without the British."

In the end the British, bound inexorably by the 1962 contract, confirmed their commitment. Indeed, there had been no escape clause. Concorde would be built *with* the British. Yet the *entente* was far from cordial. In this tense atmosphere, everything led to an argument, including the final *e* in the spelling of Concorde's name. It was not until 1967 that Anthony Wedgwood Benn, the British minister dealing with the project, accepted the presence of the *e* in both languages. Tactfully he explained that the *e* would stand for "excellence, *entente*, and Europe." The final hiccup occurred in 1970. Members of incoming Conservative prime minister Edward Heath's cabinet did not believe in Concorde, and wanted to freeze contributions to both the prototypes and the final version. It took all the diplomatic skills of Lord Rothschild and the Central Policy Review Staff to change their minds.

PARALLEL OPERATIONS

These ups-and-downs illustrate the ambiguous political intentions that emerged during the co-operative effort. To keep both the French and the British happy, it was decided from the start to construct two prototypes on two separate assembly lines using two distinct research programs developed by two industries and controlled by two governments. The specifications called for a payload of 6–8 tonnes or 60–80 passengers. The aircraft had to be able to fly fully laden for 2,175 miles (3,500 km). On the other hand, the Mach speed was left to the individual manufacturers.

In both countries, research into supersonic flight had led, in the mid-1950s, to the development of numerous military projects: the Fairey Delta in the UK, the Mirage, Gerfaut and Durandal in France. These concept aircraft were delta-winged and all capable of reaching Mach 2. Engineers now had to evaluate their weaknesses and strengths and face the challenge of perfecting a long-haul supersonic jetliner. The feasibility of such an aircraft was quickly demonstrated thanks to the work conducted in parallel by ONERA and the Royal Aircraft Establishment, Farnborough. On both sides of the Channel the first designs were being put on paper. In November 1956, British aircraft and engine manufacturers, together with representatives of BEA and BOAC, opened the show by forming the Supersonic Transport Aircraft Committee (STAC). The prototype's shape was reminiscent of the SO 9 000 Trident, with its short, straight wings and engines mounted in pods at the tips.

PAGES 30, 31
The development of Concorde was a fifty-fifty partnership between France and Great Britain. The main contractors were BAC and Sud Aviation; Bristol-Siddeley and SNECMA provided the engines. Other firms participating included Dassault, Hispano Suiza and Messier. One outcome of the "equal shares" agreement was that BAC had to design part of the fuselage, while its actual construction was carried out by Sud Aviation.

PAGES 32, 33
LEFT & RIGHT: Tracing out Concorde's wing design. The metal sheet used for the wing skins is marked up before it is sent for machining at the Toulouse factory. The design of Concorde's ogival wing was the engineers' compromise to reduce take-off and landing speeds while limiting the angle of attack.

OPPOSITE: Engineers pose with a wooden model of Concorde in the factory at Saint-Éloi.

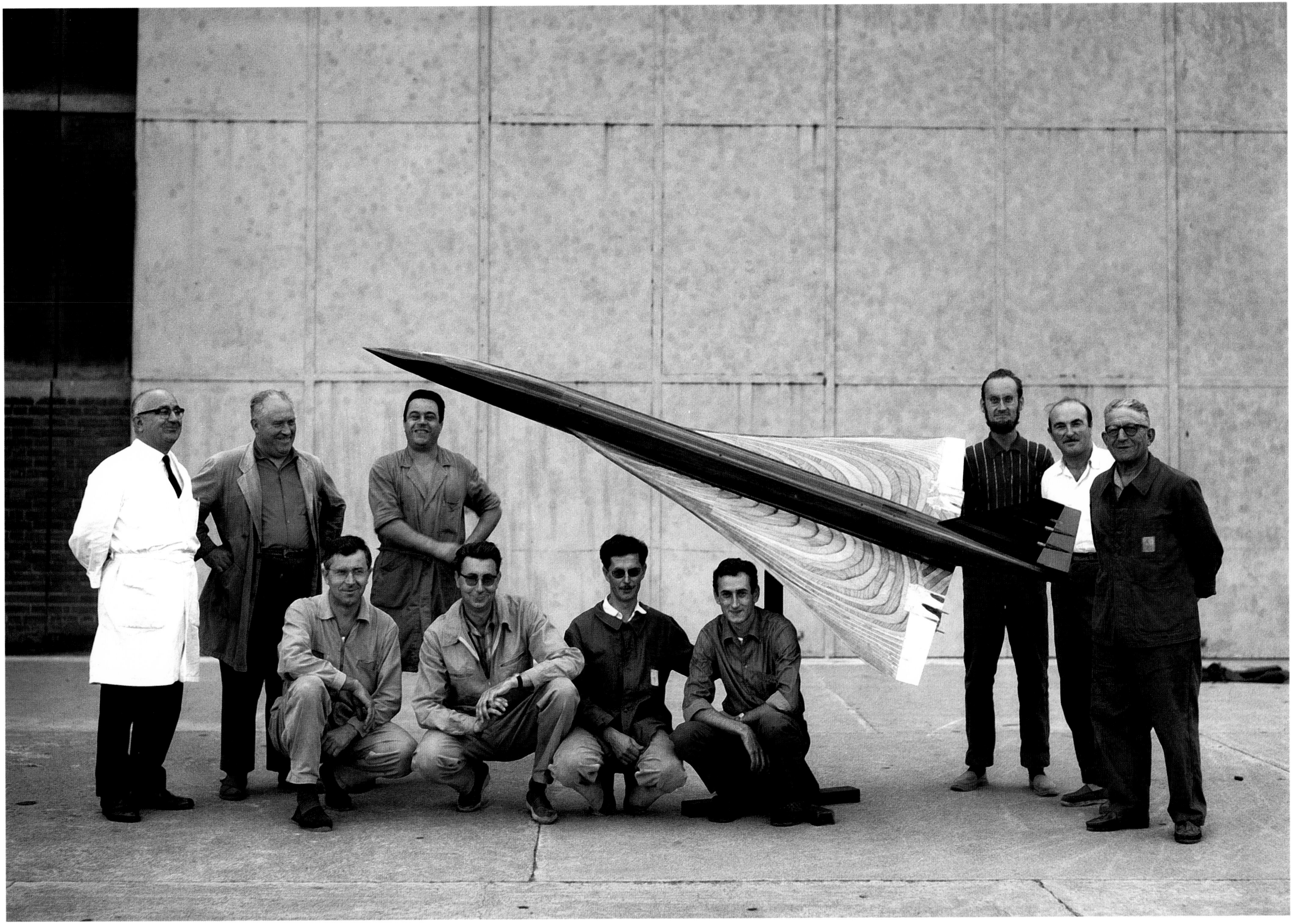

In France, a competition was launched in which Dassault took part alongside Nord and Sud Aviation. Meanwhile ONERA was researching the best wing shape, the problems of low-altitude flight and how to optimize performance at a cruising speed of Mach 2.2. The creation of STAC, followed in 1957 by the US establishment of the first Supersonic Commercial Air Transport (SCAT) program, prompted a reaction from Georges Héreil, president of Sud Aviation, the offspring of the merger between SNCASO and SNCASE. Persuaded that the Americans would succeed, he set his R & D departments to work on a supersonic airplane with the same capacity as the Caravelle. At the end of January 1958, Sud Aviation unveiled a project known as X225. This delta-winged "Supercaravelle", with her five turbojets, would carry 60 passengers at Mach 1.8 over a distance of nearly 1,900 miles (3,000 km). The Dassault blueprint on the other hand was based on the Mirage IV and copied its general design. It was to fly at Mach 2.2 with 82 passengers. Nord Aviation in turn proposed a 70-seat airliner with delta wings, four jet engines grouped under the tail-fins and a canard (fuselage-mounted stabilizer) forward. Meanwhile, in Toulouse, Sud Aviation's engineers were finalizing plans for the Supercaravelle. Originally they intended to incorporate canards as well as delta wings, but in the event opted for a design with a single vertical tail. At the 1961 Paris Air Show Sud Aviation were declared the competition winners.

On the other side of the Channel, companies were hard at work on the Fairey Delta 2, designed for studying the transition from subsonic to supersonic speeds. Powered by a Rolls-Royce Avon engine with afterburner, this aircraft snatched the world speed record as early as 1956, reaching 1,147 mph (1,846 kmh) at an altitude of 39,370 ft (12,000 m). Shortly afterwards, the Fairey Delta 2 was rebuilt as the BAC 221 after modifications to its delta wings, which left them more ogival (curved) in shape and closer to that of the future Concorde. Handley Page came up with the HP115 to explore the low-speed characteristics of the ogival wing shape. Finally, the famous aerodynamicist Dr Archibald Russell evolved a format for Bristol Aircraft Ltd. (later BAC after merging with Vickers, English Electric and Hunting). This was the BAL 198, an ambitious design with five jet engines and capable of carrying 132 passengers. But Russell came under fire for his over-optimism. He had to reduce airfoil size, ending up with a more realistic, four-engine design—the BAC 223, a 100-tonne, 100-seater aircraft. With its lowerable (droop) nose allowing a better view from the cockpit during take-off and landing, the BAC 223 looked much like the final prototype of Concorde.

THE TWO PROTOTYPES

On October 13 1961, the co-operation between BAC and Sud Aviation resulted in agreement on a definitive program for the construction of two versions of the supersonic jetliner, one for short-haul flights and the other for long-distance. These were the outcomes of two separate lines of development: the Supercaravelle and the BAC 223. Traditional civil aviation practice was to build one or several prototypes which would form the basis for the initial production model, which would in turn be the version eventually submitted for certification. But naturally Concorde formed a special case. The "equal-shares" agreement between Great Britain and France stipulated the simultaneous construction of both prototypes, then two pre-series models—all of which would extend development time. The two models bore a strong mutual resemblance. Each had four engines producing approximately 220,500 lbs of thrust on take-off, and could carry 100 passengers or 1,575 lbs (10,000 kg) of cargo. The airframe and propulsion units were to be manufactured separately. BAC, for the British, would undertake the forward section (including the cockpit), the rear fuselage, the pods and air intakes for the jet engines, plus the tail assembly. The central section of the fuselage, the wings and landing-gear were to be the responsibility of Sud Aviation. SNECMA would undertake the highly complicated exhaust nozzles system on the Bristol-Siddeley Olympus engines. To this mutual co-operation the French engine manufacturers brought the experience acquired with the Griffon and the SE Durandal and variants of the Atar 9 used to power the Mirage III and IV.

At the time, the Olympus, the 300 version of which was mounted in the RAF's subsonic, delta-wing Avro Vulcan bombers, was the only suitable propulsion unit available in Europe with real potential for development. But its adaptation for supersonic flight demanded a considerable number of further modifications, particularly to ensure the correct air intake for the engines at all speeds and angles. The fact was that at low speeds and under acceleration, the Olympus' performance had proved disappointing. To maximize output, the compressors had to be supplied with ambient air, which meant utilizing the aerodynamic effects of the wings.

OPPOSITE
Wind-tunnel test. Concorde's wings were designed to maximize low-speed lift. Note the vortices forming at the upper surfaces of the delta wings at a given angle of attack.

PAGES 38, 39
LEFT: The construction of the fuselage, including the cockpit, fell to the British.
RIGHT: Building the first production model. A technician poses on the framework that connects the wings to the fuselage.

This led to the idea of grouping the engines in pairs and mounting them in a pod beneath the wings, with the exhaust nozzle level with the trailing edge. All three major parts of the powerplant—the special air intake, the turbojet, the exhaust—were designed to be dismantled separately during maintenance and repairs. The overall structure had to be solid, but not of course rigid; the under-wing positioning of the engines meant that they had to flex with the wings, necessitating a system of joints. And to save weight, both engines and their pipework had to be incorporated inside a single pod, while remaining physically and mechanically separate. Finally, a means had to be devised to regulate the flow of gases between the three components. The engineers faced a tough challenge.

THE PRINCIPLE OF THE DELTA WING

Since the mid-1950s, British and French researchers had been of the same opinion, that the ideal aerodynamic formula for supersonic flight was a sharply swept-back, triangular wing, as thin as was practicable. The laws of physics dictate that in supersonic flight the drag of a wing increases with the square of its thickness. And the more acute the angle of sweep, the greater the efficiency at speeds above Mach 1. On the other hand, performance at subsonic speeds is reduced. But with a less pronounced sweep and a wider wingspan, the opposite occurs. To be viable and carry passengers, the future Concorde would need to take off and land at reasonable speeds, to climb and cruise below Mach 1 and maintain a holding pattern while waiting to land.

Engineers were aware that the lift of a classic delta wing falls off at low speeds. To resolve this problem, what is known as a variable geometry wing would be developed. But in Concorde's case, another solution— or rather compromise—was adopted: the triangular wing-shape with its acute sweep angle. Wind-tunnel experiments demonstrated that beyond a certain angle of attack, this shape acquired an extra 25 per cent lift owing to the vortices that developed at the upper surfaces of the wings. Better still, the same studies indicated that the more acute the sweep angle, the more stable and powerful the vortices along the whole length of the wing. Employing this solution, designers came up with the ogival wing for Concorde, a design nicknamed "High Gothic"—after the ogee or double curve employed in medieval architecture—by the ONERA engineers. This variation on the double delta incorporated two successive sweeps, each of different size and angle. The leading edge of the wing, seen in plan form, follows a sinuous curve. The steeply angled forward section increases lift by generating stable vortices at low speed. The angle of the second, mid-wing sweep is less acute; it permits an extended wingspan, improving aerodynamic efficiency at subsonic speeds. The wing tips are rounded off, giving the aircraft greater stability at steep angles of attack.

It was also important to exploit the phenomenon of lift at low speeds and to provide for the natural tendency of an aircraft to become nose-heavy on attaining supersonic velocity and the state known as hyper-stability. With fighter aircraft, which flew supersonically only for a few minutes, a pilot could level off simply by raising the trailing edge flaps, thus increasing drag. Such an option, however, was not acceptable with a civil jetliner. So an idea was borrowed from engineers who had worked on the Mirage IV: the fuel would be used as ballast. The harder an aircraft accelerates, the more its centre of aerodynamic lift is displaced towards the rear. In Concorde's case, engineers calculated that at Mach 2.2, it would move back 6 ft (2 m). To compensate for this displacement without using conventional elevators—which would increase drag—the solution was to transfer fuel from trim tanks situated forward of the centre of lift to others in the after fuselage. These tanks held a third of the fuel, the rest being distributed in the wings. While climbing and under acceleration, fuel would be pumped from the forward tanks to those in the wing and tail. This would cause the centre of gravity to be displaced aft simultaneously with the centre of lift. To give the aircraft ultimate stability, the wings were designed slightly skewed (i.e. with twist and droop), the degree of which is calculated to offer greatest efficiency around Mach 1. But while resolving one problem, this solution created another. A complicated pumping system was required, which added more weight and ate up space. To increase aerodynamic performance even further, it was decided to blend the fuselage into the wing and construct both parts in one piece. The sections of the fuselage would incorporate the wing roots, a design unique at the time in such a large aircraft. Because of the high angle of attack characteristic of a delta wing, the British decided to equip the jetliner with a lowerable (droop) nose section, a system already in use on the Fairey Delta 2. At cruising speed, to reduce drag, the cockpit canopy has to be perfectly aligned with the

42

PAGES 40, 41
LEFT: On either side of the Channel a huge logistical effort was required to transport the materials for constructing Concorde; this was the first time an airplane had been built on a continental scale. Convoys shuttled ceaselessly between Toulouse and Filton. From Aérospatiale's factory in Toulouse the trucks headed for Le Havre or Cherbourg before taking the cross-Channel ferry to Southampton.

RIGHT: To transport bulkier materials, Aérospatiale employed Boeing "Super-Guppy" 377s belonging to the French firm Aéromaritime, a subsidiary of UTA. Constructed in the late 1950s, this four-engined aircraft had originally been designed to transport rocket sections.

OPPOSITE
Concorde's airframe was made of a special heat-resistant aluminum alloy known as AU2GN. It was not new, having been previously used by many manufacturers for the construction of turbine blades. Its only drawback was that it tended to age quickly.

front section of the fuselage. But on take-off and landing, all the pilots can see is the aircraft's nose. The remedy is a nose with three possible positions: partially lowered for take-off, fully lowered on approach, landing and taxiing, and raised for high-speed flight. It is equipped with a retractable visor to protect the windshield from the heating effects of friction. At supersonic speeds, despite the cold (–67°F/–55°C) at 55,000 ft (17,000 m), the effect of the aircraft forcing itself through the air produces a sharp rise in temperature. At Mach 2.2, friction heats the nose section to 356°F (180°C), the leading edges of the wings to 311°F (155°C), and the fuselage and the trailing edge to between 284 and 302°F (140–150°C). The engineers at BAC and Sud Aviation agreed on a choice of material to counter the heat problem. They decided to use the heat-resistant aluminum alloy AU2GN—known in the UK as RR58, with reference to Rolls-Royce—already employed by several engine manufacturers for their turbine blades. The only disadvantage of AU2GN is that it tends to age somewhat rapidly. The other possibility was titanium, but this metal is heavier and harder to work. According to Archibald Russell, AU2GN is far more effective against the "heat barrier".

HARNESSING THE MIGHT OF INDUSTRY

Concorde's strategists never made a secret of their ambitions: to impress upon the world, or more precisely America, their technological superiority, to breathe new life into the British and French industries involved and to thrust aeronautical engineering into the twenty-first century years ahead of time. To meet this challenge, Sud Aviation had two new assembly plants constructed at Toulouse-Saint-Martin and re-equipped its factory at Toulouse-Saint-Éloi with all the latest tools, such as the first digitally controlled milling machines. SNECMA, who were producing the exhaust system for the Olympus 593 engines, were obliged to develop special high-temperature resistant steel. The metallurgists employed titanium-based alloys and other heat-resistant varieties based on nickel and cobalt. As in the Dassault plants, all the aluminum components were cut out in one piece to reduce deformations resulting from mechanical welding. These new materials required investment in enormous industrial resources, such as a large-capacity sheet-metal roller for the heat-resistant alloys, a massive drop-hammer, purpose-built argon and vacuum furnaces and a 3,000-tonne stamping-press.

Research centers and the wind-tunnels at ONERA and the Royal Aircraft Establishment were working round the clock. At Farnborough, a new 150-ft (45-m) tall aerostructures laboratory sprang up. At the Toulouse-Blagnac plant, as at Filton in England, sections of the central fuselage were readied for pressure and heat testing. Engineers used infrared lamps to heat the structure and simulate the acceleration phase while cooling it with air refrigerated by liquid nitrogen to mimic deceleration. Also sited at Toulouse was a huge building for testing the flight controls, hydraulic circuits, landing gear, ailerons and air conditioning system; it also housed the test beds for the fuel. A very impressive device known as an Adamson machine, the only one in Europe, was used to test aircraft tires: it could simulate acceleration from 0 to 400 mph (0–650 kmh) in less than 15 seconds and reproduce the stresses to which the tyres would be subjected on take-off and landing. Jet engines were ground-tested at Toulouse, Filton and the RAF base at Fairford, using newly constructed concrete noise suppression facilities ("hush-houses") containing a network of ducts with absorbent panels to remove the exhaust gases.

A LOGISTICAL TRIUMPH

In total, some 600 British and French firms were engaged in building components for Concorde: an aviation record. To transport all the parts to the right places demanded an intricately coordinated strategy. The French Breguet 763 "Deux-Ponts" aircraft was used to ferry the engineers and the Olympus engines between Bristol-Filton and Melun-Villaroche (Seine Maritime), headquarters of SNECMA. The fuselage sections traveled on board four-engined turboprop Short Belfasts of the RAF; the first transfer by cargo plane took place on September 1, 1966. Aérospatiale also hired two, then four Boeing 377 "Super-Guppies". The largest components were moved by road and sea; the trailers were equipped with telescopic platforms to cope with obstacles en route. The convoys of trucks crossed the Channel by ferry between Le Havre or Cherbourg and Southampton before finishing the journey to Bristol by road.

OPPOSITE
Designed in 1953 for the RAF's subsonic Vulcan bombers, the Bristol-Siddeley Olympus engine became the choice for Concorde. It was improved to give 33,000 lbs of thrust and renamed the 593.

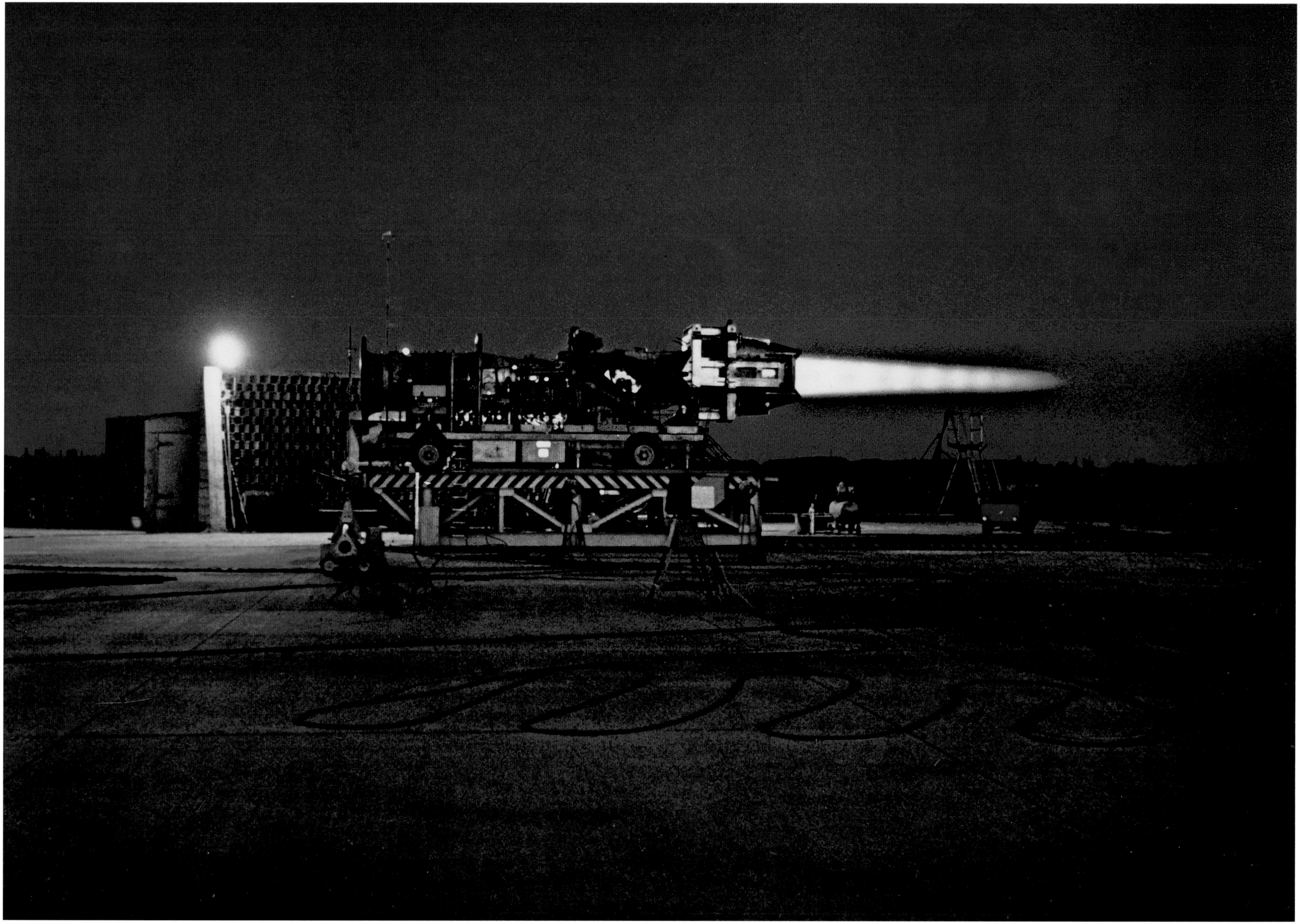

LUCIEN SERVANTY, FATHER OF CONCORDE

Born in 1909, the son of a First World War fighter pilot, Lucien Servanty was self-taught when he began his career, eventually completing his training at the Arts et Métiers engineering college. He entered the firm of Louis Bréguet in 1931; in 1937 he moved to SNCASO (Société nationale de constructions aéronautiques du Sud-Ouest, afterwards Sud Aviation and finally Aérospatiale).
The outbreak of war in 1939 could not put a brake on Lucien Servanty's creative genius and he continued to conduct his research in secret. In 1941, he developed the first all-metal glider while also pondering the future possibilities of jet propulsion. After the Liberation, he sweated blood to give France her first jet aircraft, the Triton, designed clandestinely during the war years. The Triton was swiftly followed by the Espadon and, more importantly, the Trident, the first mixed propulsion supersonic aircraft, which captured numerous world records. This remarkable talent for super-sonic design made Lucien Servanty the obvious choice when it came to developing the medium-haul supersonic airliner first known as the Supercaravelle and subsequently Concorde.

The Trident program had been discontinued in May 1958 and Servanty, then director of Sud Aviation's R & D department, found himself and his team without a job. Then Georges Héreil, president of Sud-Aviation, suggested Servanty apply his experience with military supersonic aircraft to a civil airliner with the same capacity as the Caravelle (80 seats) and a range of roughly 2,000–2,500 miles (3,500–4,000 km). This was primarily an exercise in style, but Servanty and his co-workers were thrilled. Always bold in his designs, Servanty loved a challenge and desired nothing better than new horizons to explore. At times his search for innovation had to be reined in, no easy task given his natural stubbornness. For a long time he also backed the concept of vertical take-off, as applied to rocketry. At the 1961 Paris Air Show, Sud Aviation presented its mock-up of a supersonic airliner, a concept airplane closely fore-shadowing the future Concorde with its swept-back wings and fighter-like profile. With Gilbert Cormery, his right-hand man and head of the aerodynamics section, Servanty presided over Concorde until his death in 1973, though he never flew on the

aircraft he had created. However, his obstinacy is considered by many analysts as one of the reasons why Concorde did not find the right niche in terms of capacity and range.
André Turcat paid a last tribute to Servanty during his farewell to Concorde. "We were even accused of being perfectionists; but should we have been anything less? And this is the spirit in which we worked in R & D. I can still picture Lucien Servanty, the department head, coming to inspect the flight recordings, which, at the time, were made on strips of photographic paper. Without uttering a word, armed with a slide-rule—now a museum piece but then the engineer's most valuable tool—and a pair of dividers, he re-measured every item recorded and turned it over in his mind."

OPPOSITE
Caution, slow-moving load! A fuselage section on the way to the ferry at Cherbourg.

LEFT

Concorde slowly takes shape at the Toulouse assembly
plant. Sud Aviation invested in two purpose-built buildings
at Toulouse-Saint-Martin and had to equip its factory at
Toulouse-Saint-Éloi with the latest machine-tools.

PAGES 50, 51

LEFT: French production Concordes being assembled, with
a pre-production 102 (F-WTSA) at the far end of the building.
The latter was used, along with 101 (GAXDN) to finalize the
design of Concorde. These two models underwent considerable
modifications and ended up quite unlike the Strang and
Servanty design from 1962.

RIGHT: Charlie Chaplin anticipated this scene in *Modern Times*.
Here, technicians assemble part of the wing structure.

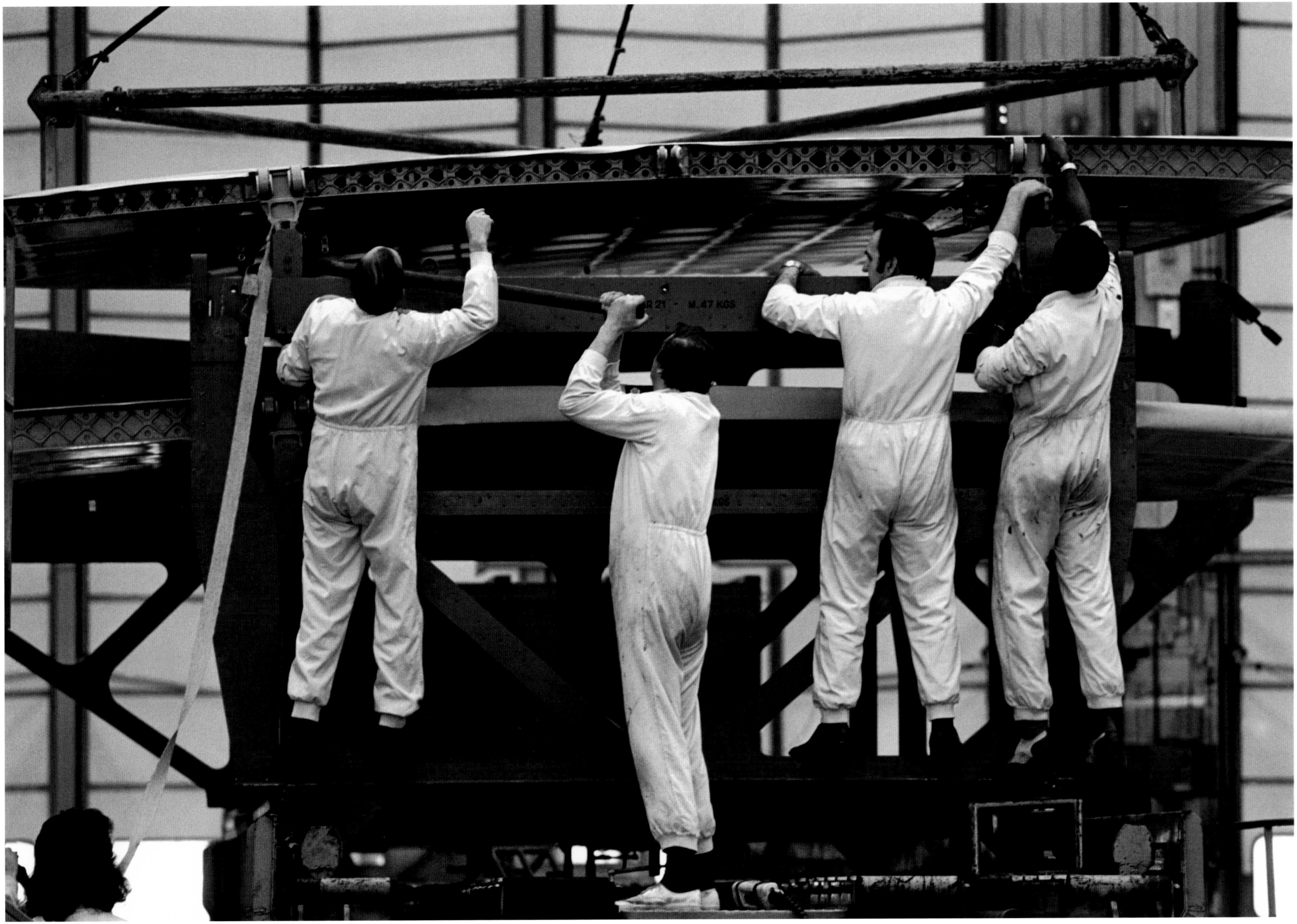
M.47 KGS

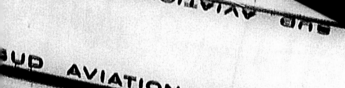

TESTS AND TRIALS

*To squander a fortune in public money, billions
and billions, stubbornly carrying on with a Concorde
we can sell only to ourselves...*

JEAN-JACQUES SERVAN-SCHREIBER, EDITOR OF *L'EXPRESS* AND MEMBER OF
THE FRENCH CHAMBRE DES DÉPUTÉS, AUGUST 28, 1972

SHOWING HER NOSE

There was a lingering fog hanging over
Toulouse on December 11, 1967, when
Concorde poked her streamlined nose outside
the hangar and made her first appearance,
free of the scaffolding that had previously
hidden her graceful profile. It was just an
opportunity to show off her lines: the select
band of attendant spectators may have
thought she would be taking to the air in a
few months, but in fact her engines weren't
even ready for ground-testing.

Returned to her hangar once more, Concorde
continued to undergo modifications and
finishing work as the clock ticked away.
Every electrical circuit and on-board
instrument was checked, one by one. Her
engines would not be started and ground-
tested until the end of the summer. The first
official taxiing trial took place on August 20,
1968; the press had been invited and packed
the sides of the runway. The program
consisted of what seemed to be very
elementary operations: releasing the brakes,
maneuvering the nose wheel (allowing the
aircraft to turn), lining up on the runway
and accelerating to just under 40 mph
(60 kph). Hardly supersonic speeds. But
the pilot was faced with a novel situation:
perched forward of the wheels, he could
only ensure he was following the line down
the centre of the taxiway by watching a
monitor picking up images from a camera
mounted on the nose wheel. Once the crew
got their bearings, however, this system was
soon dispensed with. The days passed;
Concorde was allowed to accelerate faster
down the runway, but encountered problems
with braking when the brake chute opened
too slowly.

The program was progressing slowly but
surely towards the first flight. There was
some speculation that the airplane might
take part in the Farnborough Air Show in
September 1968—but that was never really
on the cards. Incarcerated for yet more
months in the hangar while the test results
were evaluated, Concorde resumed high-speed
taxiing trials towards the end of January
1969. At the same time, the second prototype
emerged from the British factory at Filton,
Bristol. Back in France, on February 21,
in her ultimate ground trial, Concorde was
accelerated to 186 mph (300 kph) on the
runway at Toulouse and brought to a halt
without the use of the parachute or reverse
thrust. At last, a date was fixed for her
maiden flight, which would take place on
March 2, 1969, almost a year later than
initially proposed.

TO BE OR NOT TO BE?

Despite Concorde's successful flight at Mach 2,
or maybe because of it, the Americans decided
to end their own involvement in supersonic
research. On March 24, 1971, Congress refused
further funding for Boeing's rival SST program,
which was subsequently abandoned. On the
other side of the Atlantic, the initial reaction
was fairly optimistic; this would surely open
the doors of the US market to Concorde.
The British and French wasted little time and
on April 22 decided to pursue the Concorde
program in any way they could.

At the point that the abandonment of the
Boeing 2707 was announced, there were
74 Concordes on the order books, including
38 for American companies, mainly national
airlines. In practice, however, most of the
US customers would be unable to operate
Concorde as the United States had announced
its intention of forbidding supersonic
flights over its territory. Concorde's opponents
in Europe seized the opportunity to make
their voices heard and demanded environmental protection measures. A press campaign
orchestrated by Jean-Jacques Servan-
Schreiber, then editor of the magazine
L'Express, used the American cancellation
as an excuse to encourage Europe to follow
suit. Slamming the cost of the program, he
complained that the money could be better
spent on France's future; Concorde's payload
was insufficient, her range too short and her
running costs so exorbitant as to make her
nothing but a toy for "American millionaires".
In the States, several newspapers followed his
lead, insisting that the Boeing SST had been
an "industrial Vietnam". The airline bosses,
on the other hand, continued to woo public
opinion, convinced that Concorde was the
right airplane for American companies, filling
an existing and identifiable commercial
requirement. Opinion polls, especially those
conducted by Aérospatiale, revealed that the
extra speed of a supersonic aircraft would be
welcomed by hard-pressed businessmen flying
first class and prepared to pay highly.

THE ROAD TO CERTIFICATION

It was against this background of tension and
controversy that Concorde began her journey
down the long road towards her certificate of
airworthiness. The taxiing and acceleration/
braking trials had made it clear from the start
that her brakes were inadequate. Concorde's
weight had increased during modifications
and the Dunlop-manufactured discs had a
dismaying tendency to lose their shape when
their temperature rose to over 1,100°F (600°C)
as a result of friction.

PAGES 52, 53
F-WTSS, prototype 001, testing the stop-barrier at the end
of the runway; it was never needed.

OPPOSITE
Ground-testing Concorde's engines at full power. Note the
suppressor facility or "hush house" in the background; this was
specially constructed on the airfield at Toulouse-Blagnac with
two huge ducts to extract the exhaust gases.

PAGES 56, 57
LEFT & RIGHT: An anti-spin chute was fitted to Concorde
during trials but, like the stop-barrier, it proved unnecessary.

BRITISH AIRCRAFT CORPORATION - SUD
EN CAS DURGENCE
EN CAS DURGENCE

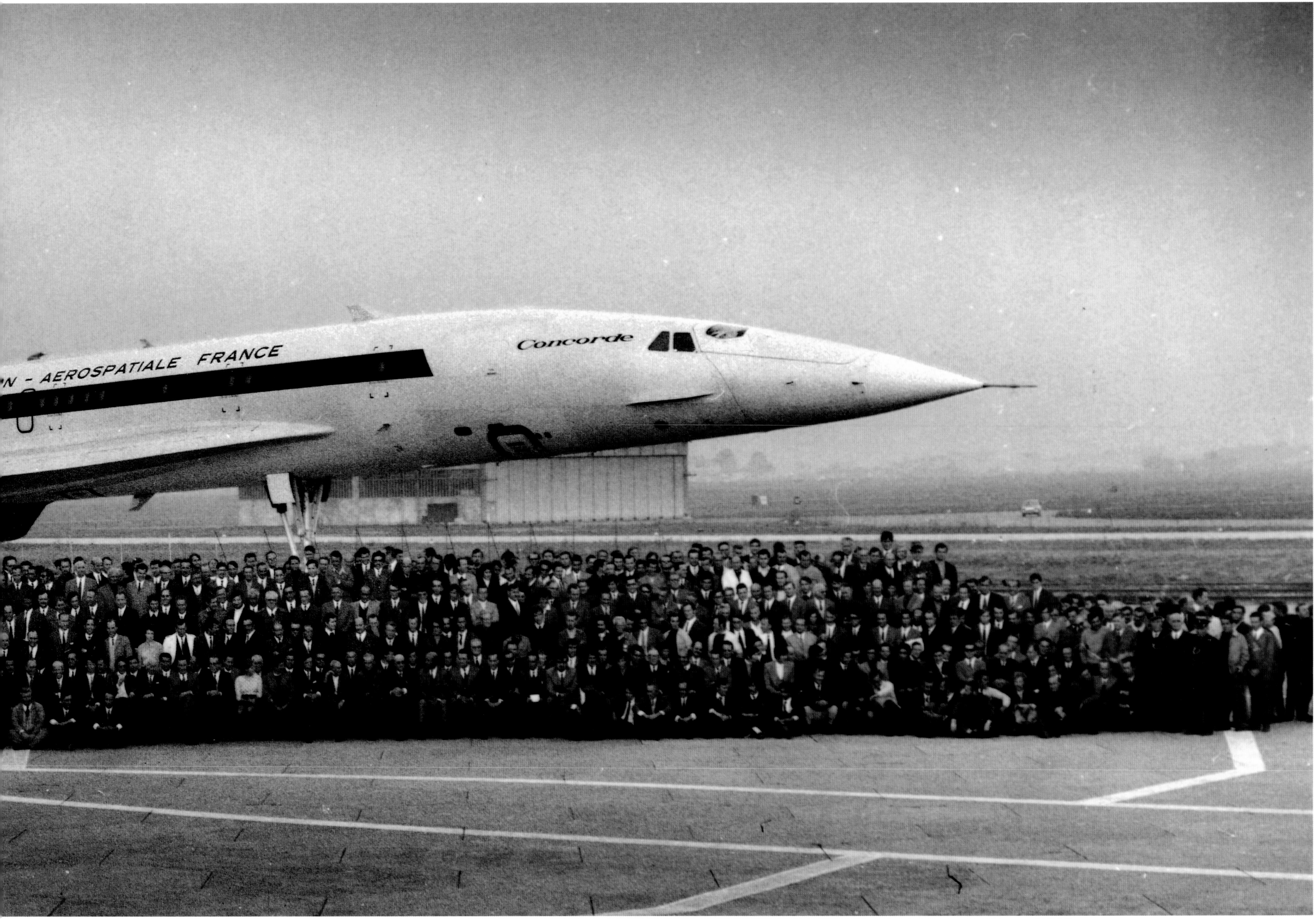
N - AEROSPATIALE FRANCE
Concorde

> *Concorde represented more than just a luxury. She remains a matter of public interest. All the hype is in the public interest.* **JEAN-MICHEL JARRE, COMPOSER, IN *LIBÉRATION*, APRIL 11, 2003**

Dunlop, who were working on carbon brakes for the USAF, suggested adapting these for the pre-series Concordes: they would be far more heat-resistant and reduce the aircraft's unladen weight into the bargain. Work on the new brakes began in 1970 and lasted until 1972. The first landings with them would take place only on August 1, 1974.

The jet engines were also put under severe strain by Concorde's increasing weight. The 001 prototype already weighed 170 tonnes instead of the 130 called for in the original design and the official figure for the first production model was 182 tonnes. The Olympus 593 engines would have to deliver 38,340 lbs of thrust instead of the original 28,600 lbs. In order to obtain this extra power, the SNECMA and Rolls-Royce engineers had to modify the air intakes and the compressors.

At the same time, US noise and emission controls necessitated alterations in the combustion system. This seriously increased the overall weight and the modifications—particularly to the afterburner units—entailed a wait while new technology was developed. Finally, to ensure optimum air supply at the intakes, the shape of the wing itself had to change.

The result was that pre-series no. 2 was very different from the prototypes and the program continued to fall behind schedule. Work on the modified engines dragged on into May 1974. But when they were installed on the production Concordes, a flutter problem once again reared its head and held up certification. The regulation of air intakes, at the root of the delay, was not completely resolved and the components not certified until November 1974.

THE SONIC BOOM DEBATE

Meanwhile other tests were in progress, giving rise to their fair share of anecdotes. André Turcat, who was in charge of these procedures, vividly recalls the installation of noise-measuring apparatus in the barn of a peasant-farmer in the Cholet region. Nicknamed "Le Canibal", it was designed to record Concorde's sonic bangs and sited under the paths of the test flights. This was a delicate subject: the growing number of bangs produced by fighter aircraft intensified public disquiet, and the tests were designed to assess whether supersonic flights would have to be conducted exclusively over sparsely populated or even deserted areas. The results demonstrated that at Concorde's cruising altitude, the bangs resulting from breaking the sound barrier were only faintly audible on the ground—though they did give local residents something of a start, providing a certain amount of ammunition to her opponents. There was also another environmental problem: the ozone layer. Concorde was not the first aircraft to penetrate the stratosphere, but it was not until her test flights that the impact on the ozone layer came under scrutiny. The French, American and British committees that collated the many measurements taken during the test flights concluded that the ozone layer was unaffected. One more obstacle out of the way! These studies also gave Concorde's French test crew the chance to make a memorable flight in pursuit of a total eclipse of the sun. Prototype 001 made her final flight soon afterwards, on October 19, 1973, landing at Le Bourget before being mothballed in the Air and Space Museum. Prototype 002 carried on for a while and underwent severe weather testing during the winter of 1973–4.

CERTIFIED AIRWORTHY—AT LAST!

From 1973 to 1975 Concorde experienced a rough ride. With difficulties over certification, orders being cancelled and a campaign by opponents to discredit her, the future looked stormy indeed. In France, a report by the Government Accounting Office clearly proposed drawing the line there and then, but the project now seemed too far advanced to be abandoned. Meanwhile in Britain, the Labour Party was once more in charge and also muttering about cancelling the project.

The prototypes had now become museum exhibits and the trials continued with the pre-series models. The British model, 101, was the first to receive the new wing design and nose geometry. Her task was primarily the resolution of problems with the air intakes and evaluation of the modified wings' performance. Her French counterpart, 102, was the first to boast all the aerodynamic features of the "series" models, including the redesigned rear fuselage and secondary nozzles. She would also test the carbon brake discs. In theory, the British and French were allotted particular areas for testing, but in practice they co-operated closely and did not hesitate to re-run each other's tests to hasten certification. Besides trials in conditions of extreme cold and heat, these pre-series models were used to investigate whether the controls would work as intended on aircraft with entirely unconventional characteristics in terms of supersonic and high-altitude flight.

61

PAGES 58, 59
On December 11, 1967, five years and twelve days after the British and French signed the agreement for the joint study and construction of a supersonic jetliner, Concorde 001 made her first public appearance outside the hangar in Toulouse before more than 1,200 people. Assembled in this group photo are representatives of the two governments, executives of the manufacturing companies and the presidents of the sixteen airlines who had taken out options on the 74 Concordes due to be built.

OPPOSITE
When the test pilots took off on Concorde's maiden flight, they already had more than 80 hours' flying experience on her under their belts, thanks to the flight simulator seen at top right.

Against this background, Concorde's makers attempted to reawaken interest across the Atlantic and persuade the American airlines to go back on the decision to cancel their orders. The pre-series versions had brilliantly proved their ability to cross the Atlantic with sufficient fuel reserves. The American public was sympathetic, but the airlines remained unconvinced. It is true, of course, that the first oil crisis had thrust the issue of fuel consumption to the fore. In 1972, aviation fuel represented 11 per cent of total running costs; by July 1974 this figure had escalated to 28 per cent following a tripling in cost. A report by IATA criticized severely Concorde's thirst for fuel: "It is regrettable that Concorde should be brought into service at a moment when neither airline companies nor customers can afford the luxury of aircraft with a limited payload but high levels of consumption and an exorbitant cost price." It was also pointed out that taxpayers were being pressured to finance the program at a time when inflation was spiraling. Nevertheless, the decision was taken to build sixteen series models. All the hopes of Concorde's backers now rested on Air France and British Airways putting her into commercial operation. But first she had to be certified airworthy. The French authorities passed her on October 9, 1975,

after some 5,500 hours of flying time—the initial plan had been for 4,000.

"We had all thought that on the very same day a British signature would confirm that Concorde was authorized to carry fare-paying passengers. It was not to be," recalls chief test engineer Henri Perrier. "In fact, during the endurance trials conducted during the summer of 1975 on Far-East routes, BOAC's pilots had convinced the British authorities that use of the automatic pilot in the conditions they encountered during high-altitude cruising presented a risk. As the automatic pilot was a French respons-ibility, we had to carry out an evaluation program in South-East Asia in November 1975. During this period we meticulously tested the equipment in the severest conditions in terms of sudden alterations in atmospheric parameters above 50,000 ft (15,000 m), such as temperature inversions and changes in wind direction. We were able to demonstrate to the authorities and future customers that by observing the proper procedures, the automatic pilot could be engaged while cruising at Mach 2 at all times with total safety."

Following these latest trials, the British certificate of airworthiness was finally granted on December 5, 1975.

During her "cold soak" (cold climate trials) in February 1974, Concorde 02 faced the snow and glacial temperatures of Fairbanks, Alaska. In the morning it was −49°F (−45°C) outside and −17°F (−27°C) inside the aircraft. The second pre-series model F-WTSA sported twin liveries: her right flank was painted in British Airways colors and her left in those of Air France.

OPPOSITE, LEFT & PAGES 66, 67
It fell to the French, in 1974, to test Concorde in conditions
of extreme cold, here and overleaf at Gander in Newfoundland.
British tests took place in hot climates. In July 1974 a
Concorde took off from Bahrain where the temperature was
117°F (47°C).

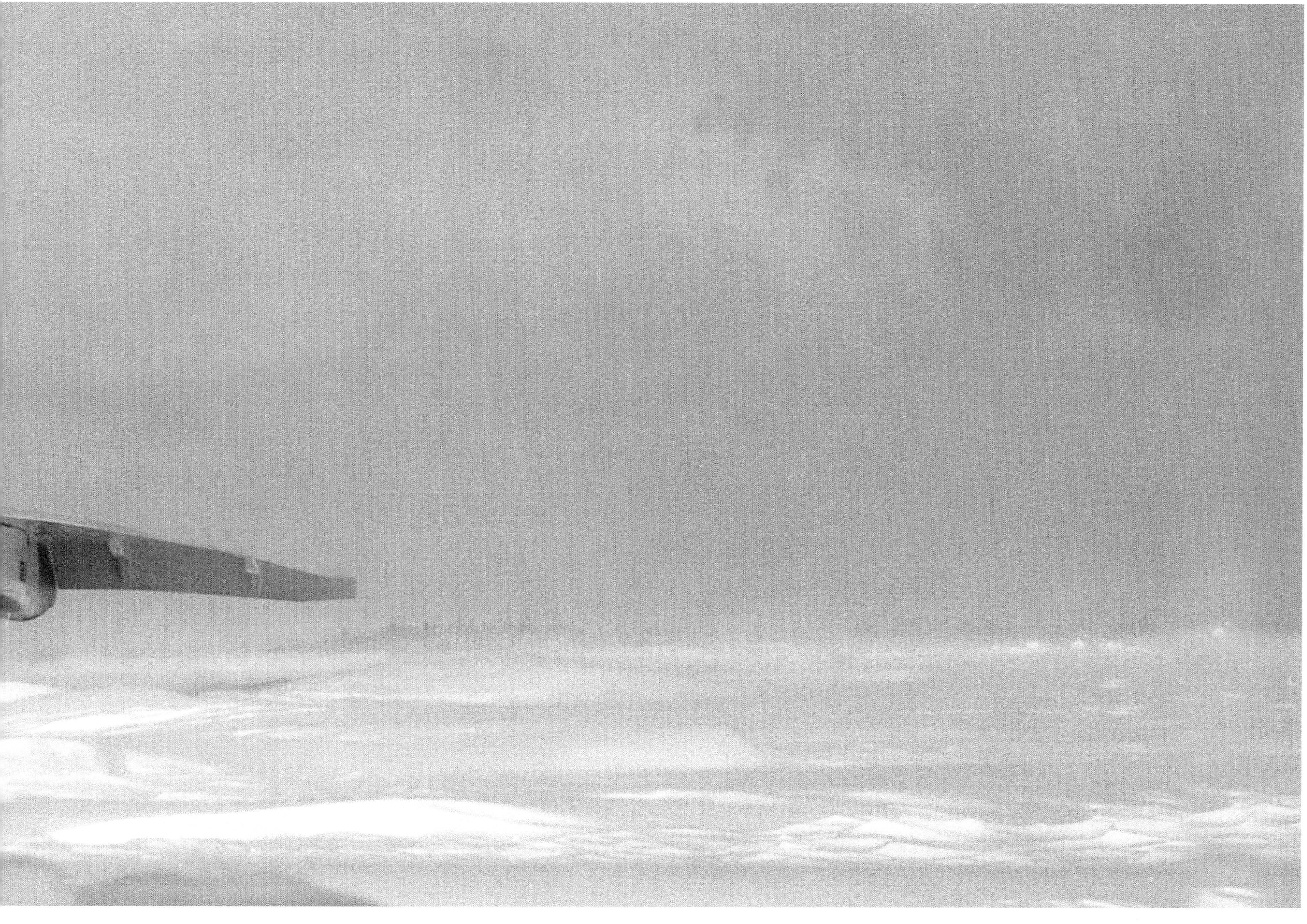

ANDRÉ TURCAT— CONCORDE'S "BIOGRAPHER"

She flies!—and she flies well.

MARCH 2, 1969, AFTER CONCORDE'S FIRST FLIGHT

On March 2, 1969, the first Concorde prototype took to the air over Toulouse. At the controls was André Turcat. He had been director of flight testing on the French side since the first day of the program and would remain with Concorde well after her commercial role was established, sharing with Brian Trubshaw, his British counterpart, the exhilaration of the aircraft's first appearances.

What future generations will remember most about André Turcat is his "biography" of Concorde, so vividly written the reader can imagine himself in the cockpit beside Turcat, holding his breath as she bursts through the sound barrier for the first time. Though with a reputation for being cold and unforthcoming, in his book Turcat manages to bring this awesome airplane to life.

The relationship between man and aircraft began six years before Concorde first left the ground. Then a test pilot on the Griffon, a fighter with proven supersonic ability, Turcat was appointed by Sud Aviation to direct the studies for what was initially conceived as the Supercaravelle program. He discovered that while the aircraft existed only on paper, the design by Lucien Servanty was sufficiently developed for him to assess what would be required of a future crew. During these six years of gestation, Turcat's role consisted in evaluating the aircraft's instrumentation, the ergonomics of the cockpit seating and procedures at each stage of flight, all for an airplane that was still on the drawing-board.

Many of the solutions developed and incorporated by Concorde's test team during this period would prove of benefit to civil aviation as a whole and advance the technology of "classic" aircraft, for instance in terms of instrumentation and simulator training. "Could you believe it? We were about to revise and modify this aircraft before she had even flown. Sometimes for reasons even the computer couldn't predict." wrote Turcat in *Concorde: Essais et Batailles*. He certainly had his share of the trials and the tribulations reflected in his book's title and moments of high emotion and euphoria, like the first time Concorde took off, her first foray through the sound barrier, the extreme weather testing, and climbing to altitudes no airliner had ventured to before.

Never blasé, Concorde's biographer turned with equal enthusiasm from analyses of the ozone layer to problems with the pilot's seat. With his rangy figure and profile reminiscent of a Roman emperor, he became almost as instantly recognizable in France as the "big bird" herself. Fittingly, after twenty-five years putting commercial prototypes and production models through their paces, this former military test pilot's last flight was aboard a production Concorde no. 7.

OPPOSITE
Artist's impression of Concorde in the livery of BOAC (later British Airways).
RIGHT
André Turcat, chief test pilot for Sud-Aviation, climbs aboard the French Concorde to perform a series of checks.

TUPOLEV OR CONCORDSKI?

Concorde wasn't the first! The Tupolev-144 took to the air on December 31, 1968, and became the first passenger jet to beak the sound barrier on June 5, 1969, and on May 26, 1970, she reached Mach 2. At the 1973 Paris Air Show, both supersonic jetliners were due to fly in public. They looked so alike that the public nicknamed the Russian design "Concordski" or "Concordoff".

The first aircraft to take off was Concorde. Her demonstration flight over, the Tupolev followed her into the air, the pilot performing a number of maneuvers to underline her capabilities. A French Mirage photographing at close quarters rose suddenly in front of her and the Tupolev took violent evasive action that resulted in her engines stalling, sending her into a dive. She broke up and hit the ground, tragically killing all on board. However, the cause of the crash is still the subject of much speculation and controversy, compounded by the fact that the black box data recorder was not found during the French investigation. One theory is that the Russians modified the flying control system overnight to produce a more impressive flight demonstration and outperform Concorde, but that a fatal error was made during these modifications. Quite apart from the speculation about the reasons for the crash, the whole future of supersonic commercial aviation now came under scrutiny.

This first blow to the project would not prove to be as serious as the later oil crisis, but it hardly helped.

What, it may be asked—apart from a demonstration of technological achievement—was the value of a supersonic jetliner to a communist country like the USSR which, officially at least, did not boast wealthy citizens hankering to be whisked at high speed to the four corners of the globe? In fact the Tupolev, of which some fifteen models were built, including prototypes, was primarily used to carry mail between the capital and outlying areas of the USSR. She carried her first passengers in 1977 on her main, and almost only, route: Moscow–Alma-Ata (Kazakhstan). But after a hundred or so flights, a Tu-144 crashed on June 1, 1978 and Aeroflot withdrew the rest of the fleet from service. Two were maintained in airworthy condition and sold to NASA in 1995 to act as laboratories for a feasibility study on a longer-range, 300-seat supersonic airliner. The project proved abortive.

There has been persistent speculation about the role of the KGB in Concordski's design; how, for instance, did the Soviets get their hands on the plans for Concorde? Others prefer to think that identical demands led to identical solutions. The truth lies somewhere in-between: the initial plans were indeed stolen, giving the Russians a head start since they now possessed the basic design. The "mole" was unmasked and put to work feeding useless or false information back to his masters. Thus the rumors of industrial espionage that had surfaced from time to time during Concorde's design stage had real substance. But a detailed examination of the two aircraft reveals more differences than might be suspected: for example, the Tu-144's wing was optimized for supersonic, not subsonic flight, while Concorde's was a compromise between the two. After the Russian model was built, its poor performance led to the installation of canards, stabilizers attached to the forward fuselage. Further, the jet engines were mounted in dissimilar fashion on the two rivals: the Tupolev's were suspended in double pods close together beneath the wings, which made it difficult to retract the undercarriage, forcing the makers to fit very small-diameter wheels. "Concordski's" career was both brief and obscure, but there is one on display today at the Automobile and Technology Museum in Sinsheim, Germany, side by side with a Concorde.

OPPOSITE
The Tupolev TU-144 bore a close resemblance to Concorde, and was nicknamed "Concordski". Her first flight took place on December 13, 1968. Piloted by Edward Elian, she circled twice above an airfield near Moscow, the flight lasting 38 minutes.

THE FIRST
FLIGHTS

OPPOSITE
In 1971, the Americans abandoned their SST program.
Opposition to supersonic flight gathered momentum,
with a campaign to ban Concorde from the USA.
On May 27, 1976, protesters demonstrated at Washington
Dulles Airport. Concorde can be glimpsed in the
background, having just made her first commercial flight.
The demonstration was a failure.
LEFT
On September 16, 1972, Concorde took part in the
32nd anniversary celebrations of the Battle of Britain.
She staged a flypast over Biggin Hill, a wartime fighter
airfield near London.

AIRBORNE!

Like all great stars, Concorde kept her fans waiting. Police struggled to organize the thousands-strong crowd as officials, reporters and spectators thronged the roof and perimeter of the Toulouse-Blagnac air terminal. This was D-day—Concorde was to take off for the first time. But the weather on the chosen day, February 28, 1969, was not co-operative. Nor on the next day. On March 2, things still seemed very much in doubt; the fog was so thick that traffic police manning intersections could not see each other.

However, the forecast did predict that conditions would improve in the afternoon: the fog would lift and the wind would remain within the parameters required for take-off. André Turcat (captain), Jacques Guignard (co-pilot), chief test engineer Henri Perrier and flight engineer Michel Rétif climbed aboard at 10.30. At 10.47 the pre-take-off check was started. But still the cloud cover persisted. The only option was to break for lunch and delay the attempt until 14.00. Despite this, the huge crowd continued to wait expectantly outside and French and British viewers remained glued to their TV screens.

Take-off checks were resumed in the early afternoon—but interrupted by an alarm.

Meanwhile, the wind was rising, threatening another postponement. But Concorde was taxiing towards the runway! You could have heard a pin drop in the crowd. At 15.40 the brakes were released. Some twenty seconds later she was traveling at nearly 190 mph (300 kmh). And "rotate"! The magic moment when the wheels leave the ground and the aircraft is finally airborne. Dramatically Concorde rose into the sky. The pilot of the shadow airplane filming her burst into an involuntary shout of delight. "You've no idea how beautiful she looks!" he cried over the radio. Years later, Concorde would arouse the same admiration among pilots waiting to take off at Roissy, Heathrow or JFK Airport. The British crew working on prototype no. 2 was on tenterhooks until she came in to land just under thirty minutes later. In his book, André Turcat relates how, when she passed over a rugby match, the referee blew his whistle and play stopped so that everyone could admire her. She flew north-west, following the river Garonne, and then made a wide turn back to Toulouse. After a graceful touchdown, she taxied gently back to the terminal's main apron to a boisterous reception from her thousands of fans. The crew met up with the "backroom boys" in the concourse for another ovation.

"As you can see," André Turcat exclaimed, "she flies!—and she flies well, I can tell you." For Turcat and his colleagues, this day marked the start of a long series of test flights. For the onlookers, a legend had already been born.

THROUGH THE SOUND BARRIER

She had indeed flown, and flown well. "The roof of the Blagnac terminal had been cleared of TV cameras, the officials and top brass had melted away from the hangars and our offices, the illuminations were turned off. But with the razzmattaz over, our activities recommenced with all the more urgency. Two days later we were due to make flight no. 2, though in the event the weather delayed it until March 8," remembers André Turcat. Concorde had not yet been tested at supersonic speeds, and there was a long way to go before she could be certified to carry paying passengers.

It was ten years since the sound barrier had first been broken, but it had never been done in the conditions and with all the constraints that faced the joint Anglo-French design. Besides the usual test flights at subsonic speeds, Concorde would have to contend with a "flight envelope" entirely new to civil airliners.

OPPOSITE
On April 9, 1969, just over a month after Concorde 001's first flight, the second prototype flew for 22 minutes between Fairford and Filton, England, with Brian Trubshaw and John Cochrane at the controls. The flight engineer was Brian Watts.

RIGHT
November 12, 1970. André Turcat at the controls of Concorde as she flies over Toulouse, paying homage to General de Gaulle who has just died.
OPPOSITE
Jean Dieuzaide's photo captures onlookers' fascination during Concorde's first public display. Her highly advanced technology aroused a mixture of admiration and incredulity.

I recall my first flight in Concorde. I'd started a six-month course on the simulator, and two-thirds of the way through I found myself in the aircraft … When I opened the throttles for the first time, it was like something I've never felt before. MIKE BANNISTER, SENIOR PILOT, CONCORDE DIVISION, BRITISH AIRWAYS

Henri Perrier, chief test engineer on Concorde's first flight recalls: "The prototype used for the first take-off was in no condition whatsoever to reach Mach 2 or even go transonic. The fuel-transfer system, in fact, was inoperative and the air intakes were still of the non-variable type." The next three years brought about considerable changes to the original design, making the test program the longest and most elaborate in the whole of civil aviation history.

Despite unfavorable weather conditions, prototype 001 flew ten or so times in the first month's testing and already demands for modifications were piling up. Thirty-eight days after her initial flight, prototype 002 took to the air with a crew consisting of Brian Trubshaw (pilot), John Cochrane (co-pilot) and Brian Watts (flight engineer). Each of the two prototypes carried over 12 tonnes of measuring equipment to evaluate performance and flying conditions. Though this impressive battery of devices enabled engineers to record four or five times as many parameters as with a conventional airplane, judgment frequently had to be exercised in interpreting the results, so novel were the context and the systems involved.

Concorde's behavior in subsonic flight was found completely satisfactory: the aircraft was stable, her controls effective and precise. She took off and landed with no particular problems and coped well with turbulence. The only trouble-spot was the braking system; a great deal of research and technical effort was needed before the engineers came up with the system employed on the pre-series models. It was now time to start nibbling away at Mach 1 and supersonic speeds.

Flight no. 45, October 1, 1969. Another big day. Besides a list of tests to be carried out at subsonic speed, the flight plan required the crew to "gradually increase speed at 35,000 ft (10,500 m) until just past Mach 1." A Mirage III would shadow Concorde to observe her behavior while a Mystère 20 would film the event for posterity. Engineers had swarmed over Concorde all during August and September re-equipping the engines with variable-ramp intakes to supply the correct quantities of air at transonic and supersonic speeds. The intakes, however, continued to plague the engineering team assigned to the problem, and the test program—which lasted until late January 1970—involved no speeds above Mach 1.5.

During this period, Concorde made fifty or so flights. She was introduced to the pilots of four of the companies that had taken out options on her—Air France, BOAC, Pan Am and TWA—and carried her first VIP, Valéry Giscard d'Estaing, then French finance minister. Finances, however, were still the biggest issue and arguments about costs grew ever more heated.

IN SEARCH OF NEW SOLUTIONS

Both the RAE and its French equivalent ONERA were devoting around 10 per cent of their staff resources to Concorde's problems: the air intakes, the flexibility of the wings—whose thin design was an aerodynamic necessity for reaching Mach 2—and coping with the heat generated by skin friction in high-speed flight. This research had important implications for the design of the structure, materials, flight controls and propulsion systems of modern aircraft. According to Philippe Poisson-Quinton, head of applied aeronautics at ONERA at the time: "The ambitious nature of the project virtually forced researchers to dream up new solutions." On February 1, 1970, Concorde returned to her hangar for the fitting of the variable-geometry air intakes and a new set of engines, more powerful and better adapted to the high temperatures arising at Mach 2. The two prototypes were withdrawn. Concorde's trek through the wilderness would last nearly eight months against a background of countless debate.

OPPOSITE
Concorde's test flight program was the longest in civil aviation history with 4,400 hours in the air, including 1,140 on the prototypes used to finalize her design.

MACH 2—AT LAST!

When Concorde took to the skies again in late September 1970, it was with a brand new propulsion system better equipped for tackling speeds around Mach 2. Conscious that all the aircraft's "firsts" so far had been French affairs, the two teams felt that this time the honor should go to the British. Henri Perrier recalls: "André Turcat and Brian Trubshaw agreed that the latter should make the attempt for the magic Mach 2 in Concorde 002. However, our British friends failed on two occasions owing to problems unconnected with the Mach number, and since we had excellent weather conditions at Toulouse, Trubshaw called Turcat and said 'Go for it!' So we did, and on November 4, 1970, Concorde 001's flight no. 102 reached Mach 2, maintaining that speed for around forty minutes. This gave us the chance to make our first assessments under the conditions for which the entire project had been designed. We were also able to record important data with regard to the temperatures of the airframe and fluids in what was the first significant step towards a simulated long-distance flight."

"We were crossing the 47th parallel," writes André Turcat, "well out to sea off Nantes and 21 minutes from take-off at Toulouse when the needle of the machmeter swung slowly from Mach 1.99 to Mach 2.00 … We held that speed for fifty-three minutes. News of our success reverberated round the world. We felt the aircraft was in her rightful element, and that we had proved it. All doubts seemed to melt away … Now we'd done this, everything else would be easy. Little did we know the tribulations that still lay ahead."

In actual fact, the extension of Concorde's flight envelope beyond Mach 2 brought to light a number of major structural deficiencies. The air intake system (again) and the design of the leading edges of the wings required modification to prevent repeated problems with flutter; on one occasion this phenomenon caused one of the variable intake ramps to break up. In early 1971 the prototypes had to be grounded once more while the necessary work was done.

STAR ON A WORLD TOUR

What better way to launch a star on her career than a grand tour? Following her test program, Concorde flew round the globe to woo prospective airline customers. Her first stopover was for the French Trade Fair in São Paulo, Brazil (1971). A group of French government ministers traveled on Concorde 001 from Toulouse to the Brazilian business capital in three stages via Cap Verde and French Guyana on a mission to promote French technology. Concorde was given a warm welcome by the Brazilians who have always had a keen admiration for things French and an eye for beauty.

During this first tour, Concorde set a number of records, including her longest yet flight (3 hours 45 minutes) and the longest flight above Mach 2 (1 hour 30 minutes). It was also the first time that an aircraft could make the France–Brazil trip and back in a single day, showing how much closer together supersonic flight had brought the continents. Concorde 002 then took over for an extensive series of demonstrations in Asia and Oceania, followed some months later by a tour of Africa.

The British team meanwhile successfully experimented with a supersonic corridor over the most deserted regions of Australia. Concorde needed to demonstrate her ability to adapt to different environments with varying characteristics.

The test crew made the most of these trips to study the aircraft's behavior under extreme conditions of heat, cold, humidity and altitude. Equally, thanks to Concorde's unique capabilities and capacity to carry the equipment necessary, these flights presented an opportunity to make scientific

OPPOSITE
Ushuaia (Argentina), February 14, 1999, 14.00. In his inflatable dinghy, Eduardo Pocai found himself at the end of the world. He was approaching Isla Conejo ("Rabbit Island") opposite Malvinas Argentinas airport to photograph Concorde landing at the continent's southernmost city, sandwiched between the Cordillera and Cape Horn. Conditions were overcast and windy. The seagulls "escorting" Concorde give the scene an almost surreal feel.

I photographed Concorde at Toulouse. I guess it was one of the first take-offs with the press present … I was standing at the end of the runway with a giant telephoto lens. Suddenly she soared up in front of me. I just managed to grab one color shot— a really great one … RAYMOND DEPARDON, PHOTOGRAPHER

observations that had never been possible before. There was no shortage of ideas for exploiting the advantages of supersonic flight; Concorde was used, for instance, to measure the depth of the ozone layer—thereby silencing those who opposed her on ecological grounds—and to follow a total solar eclipse, advancing contemporary scientific understanding of the sun.

WOOING THE WORLD—IN VAIN

The attempt to win over opinion went down far better with the general public than prospective customers. Since her unveiling at Le Bourget in 1969, Concorde and her test crews had acquired what amounted to their own fan-club, receiving mail by the sackload. As the airplane toured the world, her international following grew and grew. Wherever she appeared on the tarmac, she cast her spell; crowds flocked to watch her take-off and land. Most of them would never have the chance to go on board, but her grace and her performance won the hearts of everyone, world leaders included.

Richard Nixon rushed to see Concorde close-up during a meeting with French president Georges Pompidou who, somewhat nervously, had just made his first supersonic flight. The Shah of Iran, the Soviet Foreign Minister,

the British royal family and even the first cosmonauts all had the pleasure of breaking the sound barrier on board Concorde, adding to her notoriety among opponents but providing excellent publicity business-wise. Yet however much Concorde wowed the public and proved her capabilities as a commercial airliner, potential buyers held back—there was always some reservation or other. For the Germans and the Belgians, the problem was her lack of range. North-American airlines were not convinced of her reliability, especially since they saw the halting of the SST program in the States as proof of the non-viability of such a project. China was in favor—despite refusing to allow president Pompidou to land in Concorde on her soil —but this was counterbalanced by the non-committal attitude of Japan, where there were doubts about operating her out of Tokyo because of the range factor.

A final set of demonstrations was arranged to prove that Concorde could cross the Atlantic with a full load of passengers and fuel enough to spare in 3 hours 33 minutes on the Washington–Paris route instead of the 8 hours needed by a subsonic long-haul airliner. But American companies remained unconvinced, and it was their custom that was vital to Concorde's future.

During these operations Concordes 001 and 002 flew nearly 1,300,000 miles (2,000,000 km) to every continent, including 2,000 hours in supersonic flight. Never had an aircraft been forced to undergo such a series of extra trials in the whole history of aviation. Nor had any aroused so many differing passions. Judged purely in sales terms, the tours were a failure—but as a publicity coup for British and French technology, they had to be considered a success. It was, in the modern idiom, "an image-building exercise".

CHARTER FLIGHTS

To improve Concorde's profitability, both Air France and British Airways evolved a formula of charter flights running side by side with scheduled commercial operations. As well as the extra revenue, there was an invaluable spin-off in the form of publicity. In 1977 charter flights by Air France accounted for 155 hours of flying time, rising the next year to 219, then 270. Concorde landed at Cairo, Casablanca, Teheran, Marrakech, Pointe-à-Pitre (Guadeloupe), Colombo and Bahrain. On September 14, 1984, a special flight took place from Nice to Washington, while on February 13, 1985, the first London–Sydney charter made the journey in 17 hours 13 minutes.

OPPOSITE
Prototype uniform for Braniff hostesses to wear on Concorde. In late 1976, Air France and British Airways attained passenger load factors of 80 per cent and 94 per cent with the aircraft. As a result, the Dallas-based Braniff International, one of the

companies interested in buying Concorde, embarked on a joint feasibility study with BA and Air France for a more or less daily flight between Washington and Dallas. This would reduce flying time between London and Dallas

to 6 hours 30 minutes, half that required for a direct flight by conventional aircraft. An agreement was signed in February 1977, but the various US federal agencies still needed convincing.

On March 28 of the same year, Concorde reached the Cape in 8 hours 8 minutes. On November 8 ,1986, on the initiative of the Swiss travel firm Kuoni, BA introduced round-the-world trips taking sixteen days, via New York, San Francisco, Honolulu, Guam, Hong Kong, Bali and Cairo. On December 2, Air France followed suit with a time of eighteen days. Leaving Roissy-Charles-de-Gaulle, F-BVFF flew via New York, Auckland, Honolulu, Papeete (Tahiti), Djakarta, Bangkok, Colombo and Bahrain before returning to its departure point after 34 hours 52 minutes spent airborne, including 17 hours 58 minutes above Mach 1. There followed other round trips on which a number of speed records were broken. In March 1987, for example, Concorde completed a round trip of 26,629 miles (42,854 km) in 31 hours 57 minutes. In 1992, over October 12–13, F-BTSD set a new speed record traveling west to circumnavigate the globe in only 32 hours 49 minutes and 3 seconds. Official records include both periods in the air and stopovers; actual flying time was 23 hours 10 minutes and 44 seconds, with 18 hours, 29 minutes and 35 seconds at supersonic speeds.

A similar dash was made in an easterly direction on August 15–16 1995 by Concorde F-BTSD in a mere 22 hours, 39 minutes and 21 seconds flying time; she flew supersonically for 18 hours, 40 minutes and 8 seconds.

These two speed-record attempts were financed by the American aviation lawyer and consumer advocate Donald L. Pevsner from Miami, president of Concorde Spirit Tours. In addition to the round-the-world trips, agencies such as Club Prestige International in France and Goodwood Travel Ltd. in Britain organized "champagne flights"—or "flights to nowhere" as the Americans called them—giving passengers their first experience of supersonic travel. These round trips over the Atlantic or the English Channel were seized on by enthusiasts eager to experience Mach 1 or 2. A typical flight would last roughly 1 hour 30 minutes, and the price was reasonable compared with a scheduled flight to the States. A number of multinational companies also chartered Concorde. Towards the end of March 1996, Concorde no. 213 (Air France F-BTSD) was repainted in the livery of the soft-drinks manufacturer Pepsi, using 79 US gallons (300 liters) of paint and involving 2,000 man-hours. The transformation complete, in her new red, white and blue colors she then made a grand publicity tour of Europe and the Middle East, offering "taster" trips at each stopover. It was a brilliant media ploy.

AN AIRCRAFT FOR A QUEEN—OR A PRESIDENT

Presidents Georges Pompidou, Valéry Giscard d'Estaing, François Mitterand and Jacques Chirac regularly used Concorde, France's pride and joy, for official trips. Although General de Gaulle was one of the original instigators of the Concorde project and a staunch supporter from its inception, he never traveled on the aircraft as head of state, having left office in 1969 a few months after the prototype's first flight. In Britain, Prince Philip was the first member of the royal family to fly Concorde in January 1972, Queen Elizabeth II took Concorde to Barbados in 1977 and on three subsequent occasions to the Near East, and in 1985 the Queen Mother flew out over the Irish Sea as an 85th birthday treat courtesy of British Airways. Concorde has also flown several British prime ministers. James Callaghan became the first "supersonic prime minister" when he flew to Washington in 1982. Margaret Thatcher flew Concorde to Expo 86 in Vancouver and John Major took Concorde to Washington for a meeting with Bill Clinton in 1995. Tony Blair was one of the first passengers to fly Concorde when flights resumed after the crash at Gonesse in 2000.

On the French side, Valéry Giscard d'Estaing visited the United States in 1976 to attend the bicentennial Independence celebrations; the Concorde carrying him touched down at Washington, Philadelphia, Houston and New Orleans. But it was François Mitterand who was the most consistent presidential passenger during his two seven-year terms in office.

Many world leaders and celebrities have experienced the thrill of supersonic flight, including, in 1973, the Shah of Iran; Iran Air, in fact, had at one stage expressed an interest in purchasing Concorde. The Shah, himself an experienced airline pilot, made his own test-flight. And in 1989, Pope John Paul II flew on Concorde between Reunion and Lusaka, Zambia.

OPPOSITE
September 2003, over Heathrow, London.

PAGES 86, 87
LEFT: Photo taken during the special flight to observe the solar eclipse on August 11, 1999. Co-pilot Éric Célérier recalls, his memories still vivid: "As Concorde entered the eclipse zone, the sky gradually darkened. The sun's light became so weak we had to switch on the instrument lighting as if for a night flight." RIGHT: August 19, 2003, Heathrow: British Airways Concorde G-BOAD leaving for New York.

THE MIRACLE OF CONCORDE

It is not unreasonable to look upon Concorde as a miracle.

BRIAN TRUBSHAW, CHIEF TEST PILOT, 1967

The man who wrote these words was himself in large measure responsible for the miracle. In his two books, *Concorde: The Inside Story* and *Test Pilot*, Brian Trubshaw offers a unique insight into the development of the aircraft and his role as test pilot for the British Concorde.

Born in 1924, Brian Trubshaw was educated at Winchester, where he captained the Cricket XI. At the age of ten he fell in love with flying after witnessing the Prince of Wales's aircraft land on Pembrey Beach, near his home. When he was eighteen he decided to join the RAF; he did his training in the United States and was posted to Bomber Command in 1944. Regarded as an exceptional flier, he was transferred in 1946 to the King's Flight, which provided transport for the royal family. After a spell (1949–50) as an RAF instructor, he joined Vickers-Armstrong as test pilot on the Valiant Bomber, rising to chief test pilot in 1960 and director of test flights six years later. On two occasions he succeeded in bringing prototypes home despite their dangerous condition resulting from in-flight structural problems. Well known for his association with Concorde, he also carried out tests on the engines of the Valiant bomber, which at the time carried Britain's first atomic weapon. Immediately after the signing of the Anglo-French agreement for the project, BAC's chairman George Edwards head-hunted Trubshaw as test pilot. From that moment on he devoted his life to the aircraft. Trubshaw's energy, commitment and passion made a huge contribution to Concorde's success. He had the ear of the royal family and the knack of saying the right thing at the right time to restore hope and confidence in the program. In *Concorde: The Inside Story*, he recounts the "magical flight" from Filton, Bristol, to RAF Fairford from where he had taken off on many of his wartime missions. But he often missed out on Concorde's "firsts": when the British prototype was not ready on time, his sense of fair play would not allow him to hold up the test program and he very graciously ceded to his French opposite number, André Turcat, the privilege of making the first flight at Mach 2.

He ended his career as divisional director and general manager of the Filton works of British Aerospace from 1980 to 1986, though he remained a member of the board of the Civil Aviation Authority until 1993, also continuing to work as an aviation consultant. To mark Concorde's thirtieth birthday, he took part in a commemorative flight—this time as a passenger. A year later he was to be profoundly saddened by the disaster at Gonesse. Angered by subsequent derogatory comments about the aircraft, he sprang to her defense, describing her as "the safest airplane I ever flew."

He died peacefully the following year, at the age of seventy-seven.

RIGHT
To reduce noise emission, 30 seconds after take-off the landing gear was raised and the afterburners shut down. Concorde would be on her way across the Atlantic, landing less than 3 hours 30 minutes later in New York.

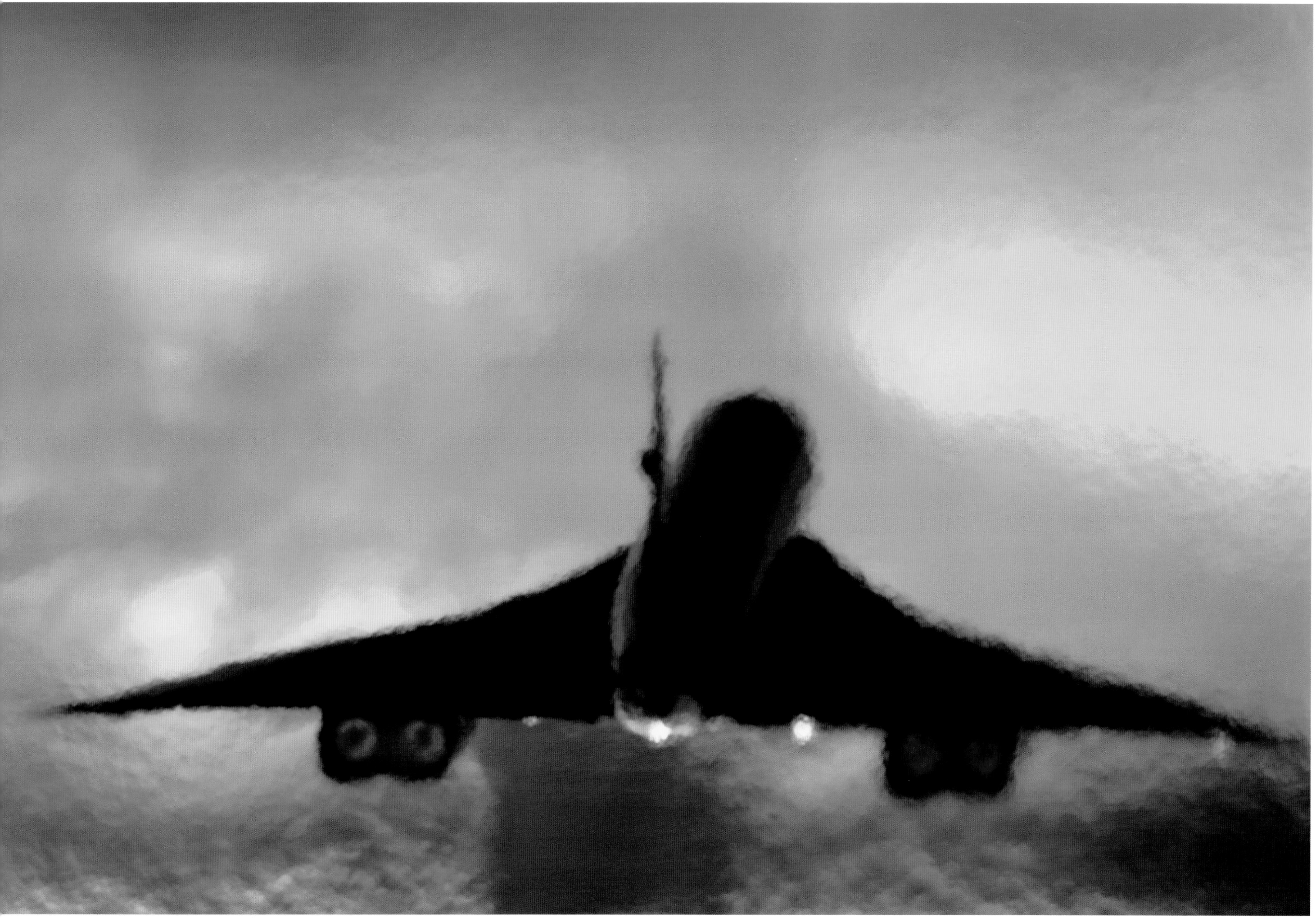

A FLYING LABORATORY

The world's fastest airliner has also served as a flying scientific observation laboratory. On June 30, 1973, an international team of some thirty researchers boarded prototype 001, then reaching the end of her career, to study an eclipse of the sun over Mauritania. By chasing the path of the eclipse, Concorde remained in the moon's shadow for 74 minutes, ten times longer than observers on the ground.

In order to enter the zone of totality at the precise moment when the moon passed between the earth and the sun, Concorde had to take off from Las Palmas in the Canaries a few minutes before the eclipse was scheduled to take place; training flights had tracked the sun on five previous occasions as a rehearsal for the real thing. André Turcat was at the controls. Four special silica quartz observation windows had been inserted in the upper fuselage to enable the scientists to carry out their observations, which were principally to study the solar corona, the chromosphere and infrared emissions in the upper atmosphere. The flight later became the subject of several scientific articles. A similar event took place on August 11, 1999, this time involving two Concordes, one chartered by British scientists, the other by the French Association d'astronomie.

The French pilot on this occasion was Jean Prunin. He calculated the aircraft's course to intersect the widest path of totality, with the advantage of a long left-hand bank, so diminishing the sun's apparent height. Passengers on one side could observe the eclipse, those on the other the shadow on the earth's surface. Concorde was traveling at 1,367 mph (2,200 kmh), the shadow at 2,050 mph (3,300 kmh); she was able to remain in the continuously moving shadow for 8 minutes and 10 seconds. Unfortunately the windows, designed to protect passengers from harmful rays, had not been modified, so no proper scientific data could be obtained —although some breathtaking photographs were shot.

Among other scientific missions undertaken by Concorde was a study of the ozone layer, which she was suspected of damaging. A Concorde crammed with sensors was flown to the North Pole; she then retraced her course to measure its effect on the atmosphere. But nothing conclusive emerged. In 1997, Concorde also detected a solar flare. During one transatlantic flight, Jean Prunin noticed the Geiger counter becoming more and more frantic as the aircraft gained altitude. His report of January 9, 1997, anticipated the official detection of the event by one day. Concorde also tracked another kind of cosmic radiation. Early in 1977, particle physicists and cosmologists had suggested installing an emulsion chamber in the hold of a Concorde. An emulsion chamber is a kind of multi-layered sandwich consisting of lead plates and X-ray film capable of detecting high-energy particles. When protons arriving from space collide with the upper atmosphere, they release cascades of particles at around 56,000 ft (17,000 m)—Concorde's cruising altitude. By October 1978, a particle detector built by Japanese scientists had been installed on Air France Concordes. For some ten years, while passengers enjoyed their champagne and caviar in blissful ignorance, the device continued to record the most spectacular phenomena, such as "jets" of extremely high-energy gamma radiation in the stratosphere.

OPPOSITE
Scientists found Concorde an exceptionally useful research tool and their experiments so cost-effective they frequently called for them to be repeated.

THE PRICE OF PRESTIGE

Concorde enabled France to be taken seriously in the world of international aviation.

PIERRE CLOSTERMAN, DISTINGUISHED SECOND WORLD WAR FIGHTER PILOT

The last Concorde was delivered in 1980. With this sixteenth model, production stopped. Costlier to operate and less profitable than anticipated, she was an economic failure. On the other hand, in terms of commerce and technical innovation, she paved the way for the future success of the European aeronautical industry, particularly the Airbus program.
Analysis of Air France's first two years of commercial operations with Concorde revealed an average "passenger load factor" of 56 per cent. After a frenetic start on the Rio de Janeiro route, the figure dropped to around 65 per cent, while for Caracas it never exceeded 40 per cent—not enough to make the operation profitable, especially as the aircraft flew little more than three hours a day, whereas seven or eight hours' service were needed to break even. A number of destinations in South America were studied, then abandoned. Singapore Airlines expressed interest, but India vetoed supersonic flights over her territory, as did Malaysia some months afterwards. A projected Tokyo service also fell through, this time due to the

intransigence of the Soviets; after the catastrophe of the Tupolev-144, supersonic flight was definitely not in vogue in the USSR. In March 1979, British Airways announced a cumulative deficit of £36,000,000; Air France's losses had reached 225,000,000 francs, excluding interest charges and depreciation (approximately $17 million and $53 million respectively, at 1979 exchange rates).
The British and French governments both gave a last fillip to their companies, but Concorde's opponents were growing ever more vociferous. "Is Concorde profitable?" wrote André Turcat. "Profitable for whom? It depends how you look at it; from the viewpoint of the airline company selling the tickets and operating the aircraft or in the more generalized perspective of the gross national product and the benefit to the country as a whole. We're talking about completely different scales and objectives … Strictly speaking, Concorde will have cost everyone in France 30–35 francs ($7–8) per year for ten years. Even then, that's cheaper and more profitable than subsidizing the coal industry … The sale price is calculated on the basis of 100 aircraft produced; you need to

have built 35 before you stop losing money and 65 more to make up the loss. As the aircraft is now, we won't sell that number. We need to get her engines and airframe right, open up new markets by giving her a longer range and make her acceptable world-wide by reducing noise emissions even further." Nonetheless, Concorde's operation did become profitable in 1983, depreciation and interest charges excluded, of course. The reason for this miracle? Charter flights.

PAGES 94, 95
LEFT & RIGHT: October 24, 2003. In an impressive tribute, Concorde is escorted over the English Channel on her last flight by a formation of the Red Arrows. Mike Bannister, senior pilot for BA's Concorde Division, recalls another escorted flight: "I had the honor of piloting Concorde during the Queen's Golden Jubilee. We flew over Buckingham Palace with nine aircraft from the Red Arrows. It was amazing, with a million people watching. I'd never seen such crowds."
OPPOSITE
To mark ten years of commercial operations and 71,000 flying hours, British Airways flew a formation of four Concordes on January 21, 1986.

A SPECIAL FLIGHT —IN EVERY SENSE

For the passengers, it's the long-awaited day—they're already at the terminal checking in. These special flights are almost always packed, and there's a holiday atmosphere right from the start. The mood is one of excitement and fun—with a tinge of apprehension. The usual procedure is to park the aircraft on the apron and bus the passengers out. Cameras are already clicking as the cabin crew show people to their seats. Doors shut; beginning to taxi. Safety briefing. Lining up on the runway. Still on the ground, but the show's already started!

Lined up ready to go, accelerating … rotation speed and take-off! A surge of adrenalin. A stunning experience given the power developed by the four jet engines with their afterburner systems. No-one speaks: the passengers' attention is riveted on what's happening. It's spellbinding stuff.

End of the initial climb. Reducing power. Resume climbing, seeking an exit point to allow the aircraft to head out over the sea and break the sound barrier. Exit point reached; afterburners reignited, acceleration,

Mach 0.99, Mach 1.00 … Cameras are clicking madly now and a cheer goes up as the mach-meter indicates supersonic flight. Time to serve the champagne and loosen up tongues. Let the good times roll! Way up at this altitude, I always reckon to have a better take on everyday life. Domestic and professional problems seem to melt away; the passengers are relaxed and laughing, probably making all sorts of plans. Thanks, Concorde.

Lunch will shortly be served. Approaching Mach 2. The sky is an even deeper blue, the ground still further away! After lunch the passengers can leave their seats and sneak a distant glimpse of the cockpit. Everyone receives a personalized certificate signed by the captain to commemorate breaking the sound barrier.

The only problem is that the faster we fly, the sooner we're back on the ground! Pulses race again as she reduces speed on approach. A slight vibration … Is she unhappy at low speeds? Not a bit. She rears like an eagle with claws outstretched; smooth touchdown, sure and safe braking. Taxiing back to the arrival

gate, a farewell message, gliding to a halt. People linger in their seats; there's no hurry to be first out.

A last photo session and time to return to homes and loved ones. The sparkle in their eyes tells it all.

Frank Debouck, head of special operations, Air France.

OPPOSITE
In March 1996, Air France Concorde F-BTSD was repainted in the livery of the soft-drinks manufacturer Pepsi who sent her on a publicity tour of Europe and the Middle East. It took more than 79 US gallons (300 liters) of paint and 2,000 man-hours to transform the aircraft. The wings were left unpainted because of possible heat problems with the fuel tanks; dark colors would absorb too much sunlight. Here, at Dubai, Concorde swelters in temperatures of 113 °F (45 °C).

LIFE ON BOARD

> *Concorde is like a great wine; you dream of it beforehand,*
> *you savor it while drinking, and remember it for the rest of your life!*

PHILIPPE FAURE-BRAC, VOTED WORLD'S BEST WINE STEWARD, 1992

A SHOWCASE OF MODERN DESIGN

Concorde's passengers were not just run-of-the mill customers. Throughout their experience they were treated like VIP guests, with their own plush departure lounge and the best wines and champagnes available in flight. Concorde was designed to mimic the luxury once found on the great transatlantic liners—everything down to the smallest detail had to be perfect and memorable. For the French version, the initial cabin styling was entrusted to a guru of 1970s industrial design, Raymond Loewy. His influence could be seen everywhere, even in the famous lunch trays which would inspire future generations of designers and change hands among collectors for astronomical sums. Concorde's décor was given a makeover in 1988 by one of his pupils, Pierre-Gautier Delaye; though never an icon like his mentor, he nonetheless made his mark in the world of design. Five years later, a complete modernization of the aircraft's interior called for a rethink. Andrée Putman, an ambassador of French good taste, noted for her work on Morgan's Hotel, New York, and Bordeaux's Center for Contemporary Arts, was invited along with a number of haute couturiers to orchestrate the new look. To mark the arrival of the millennium, Concorde undertook a world tour of New Year celebrations, refurbished for the occasion by a team from Radi Design. She now boasted the same de luxe fittings as other aircraft in the fleet and would undergo no further alterations right up to her final flight.

On the British Airways fleet, thanks to a makeover conceived by Sir Terence Conran and the London-based Factory Design, passengers would discover a superb new look when Concorde was returned to service in November 2003; features included lights that rippled through the cabin on breaking the sound barrier and new, lighter cuisine, cashmere blankets and "spa bathrooms".

For Air France, porcelain dinner services and solid silver cutlery all bore Concorde's monogram, their classical style replacing Raymond Loewy's more original but less "noble" design. Even the ashtrays were made of silver. The meals on the British Airways Concordes were served on Royal Doulton bone china with crystal champagne flutes set on Irish linen table cloths and accompanied by silver cutlery, although this had to change to plastic after the terrorist attacks of 9/11. Even the boxes of matches supplied on board were special, customized with pictures of the aircraft. All the cabin crew's equipment—thermos flasks, etc.—were numbered and stamped with the Concorde mark; the humblest corkscrew was a work of art. Today collectors do battle over pieces of the china service with its stylized representations of BA's Concorde as a big, blue bird. Throughout her years of service, the uniforms of Concorde's flight attendants were designed by some of the best couturiers available on both sides of the English Channel. The designers of the British Airways uniforms included Clive Evans, Hardy Amies, Baccarat Wethrall, Julien Macdonald and Roland Klein. Air France's uniforms, designed by Carven, Dior, Balenciaga, Nina Ricci and Christian Lacroix, were the embodiment of French chic. Nina Ricci came up with the exclusive design for a skirt matching the colors of Concorde's passenger cabin, while Angelo Tarlazzi, then a stylist with Patou, designed a summer uniform.

A TABLE UNDER THE STARS

Passengers could choose their meals from a menu worthy of the best restaurants; the cards were decorated either with simple colored silhouettes of Concorde or original designs, for example by Christian Lacroix. For every special occasion, like the millennium New Year tour, there was a different souvenir menu. The finest was undoubtedly that for the 1987 world tour with its reproductions of nineteenth-century lithographs. The wine

OPPOSITE
A full scale mock-up of Concorde on display at the Paris Air Show, 1973. The light aircraft dwarfed by her nose is a Morane-Saunier 880 Rallye.

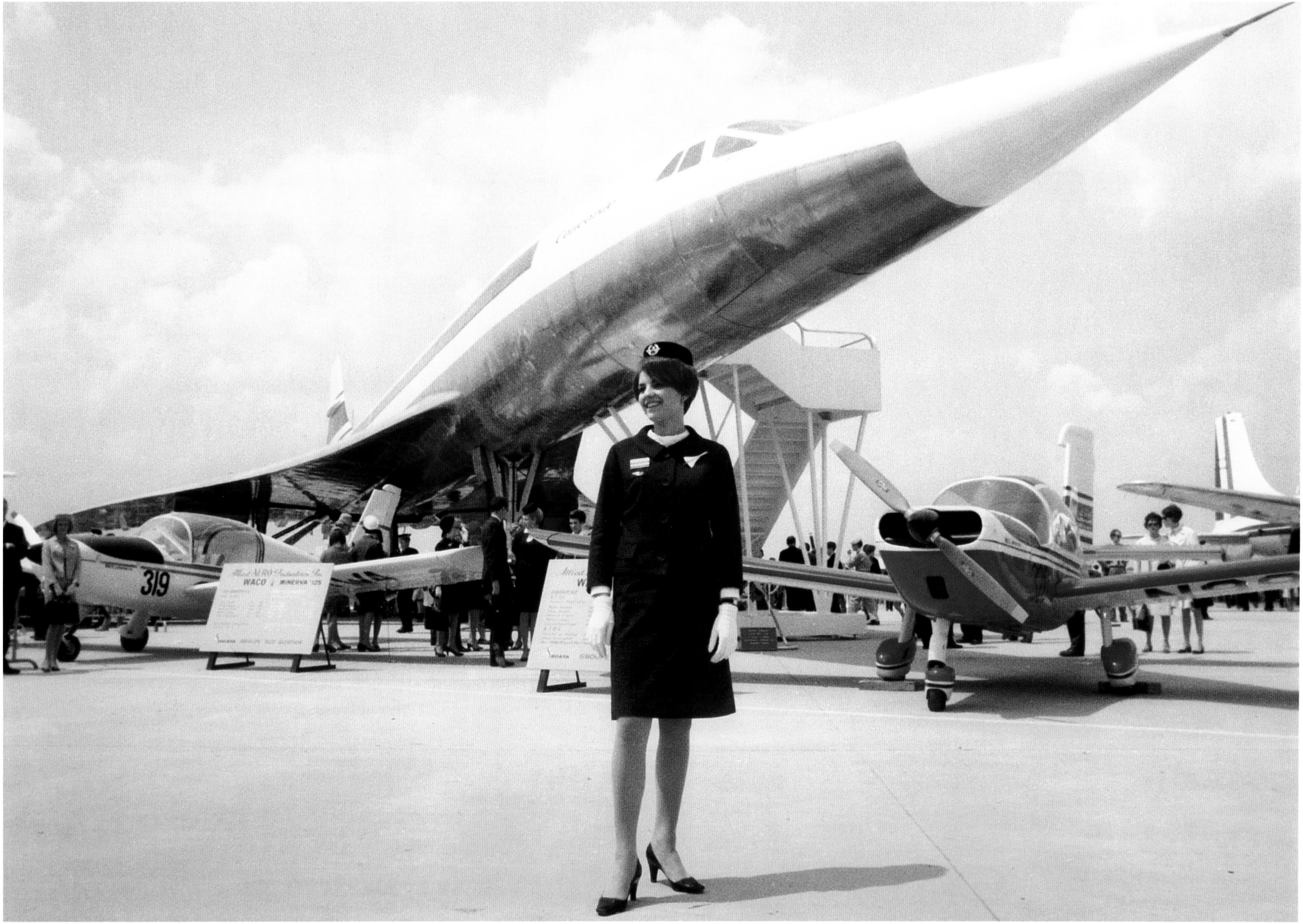
319
WACO
MINERVA 125

RIGHT

From a brochure explaining Concorde's cabin layout (early 1980s). The aircraft's interior was described as follows: "Cabin: the passenger cabin is 129 ft (39.32 m) long. The theoretical maximum number of seats is 128. However, Air France has reduced the capacity to 100, allowing more space between rows. Each row of four seats is arranged in pairs on each side of the centre aisle. The cabin is divided into two compartments separated by the toilets and cloakrooms. The forward compartment comprises 40 seats in 10 rows; the second, 60 seats in 15 rows. The front few rows in each compartment are reserved for non-smokers. Two further toilets are available at the front of the forward compartment. Seats: these are of a new type; with their high backs, all-round support and shaped and supportive neck-rests, they are specially designed for supersonic flight and Concorde's cabin. They can be reclined as required and there is ample room between each row for passengers to stretch their legs in comfort. Owing to the narrower cabin, our seats are not as wide as those customarily found in first class, but they are at least as comfortable and boast all the latest technical advances in this field."

OPPOSITE

A machmeter in the cabin informed passengers when they were breaking the sound barrier or approaching Mach 2. Environmental conditions in the upper atmosphere, however, sometimes kept Concorde at Mach 1.9. Every passenger flying faster than sound was presented with a personalized certificate at the end of the trip.

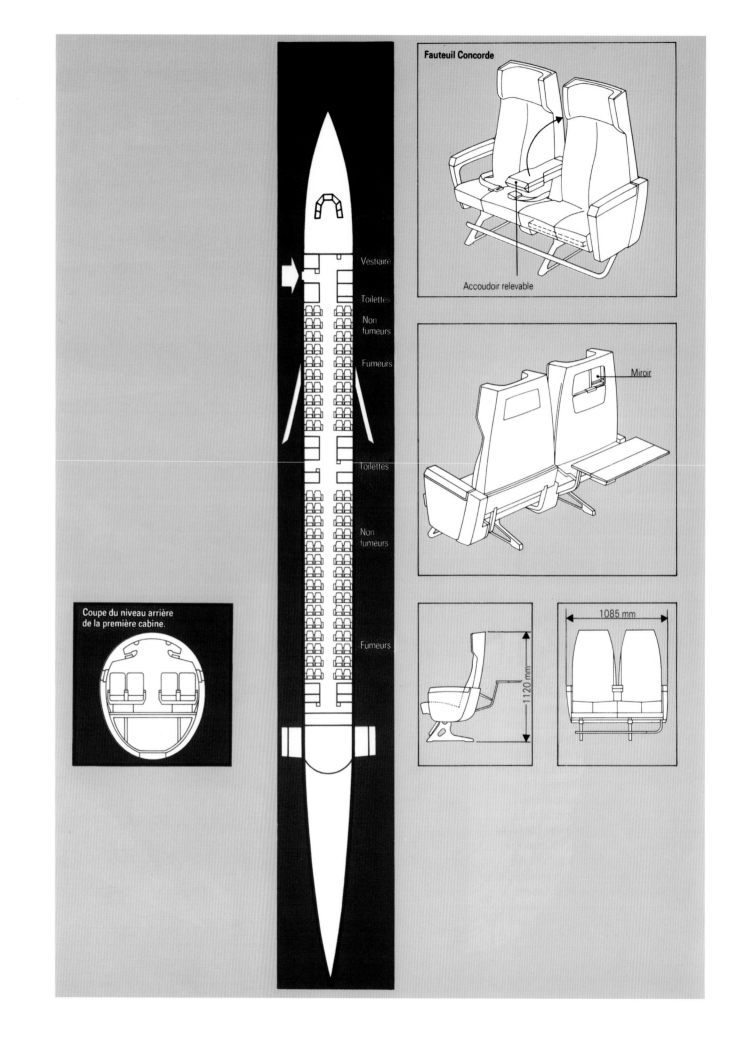

LEFT & OPPOSITE
Concorde's menu offered a possible eight courses, including coffee, with passengers free to choose dishes in any order. Meals were served from five trolleys specially designed to negotiate the aircraft's narrow centre aisle. There were six stewards or stewardesses. The 100 meals served on board, plus drinks and place-settings, represented a weight of over 3,000 lb (1,400 kg)—the equivalent of seventeen passengers.

Success involves going beyond what is reasonable.

ALAIN DUCASSE, LEADING FRENCH CHEF

list was sumptuous: every page contained a color photo of a label from one of the bottles served on board paired with a description of the wine in English and French. There were champagnes, red wines, white wines, in a host of great vintages to suit all tastes.

In the case of Air France, Concorde's in-flight meals were prepared a few hours before take-off by Servair's team of nineteen chefs and pastry cooks assisted by forty chefs from "Les Toques du Ciel" (Sky Chefs), a team specially trained by Alain Ducasse. Dishes served in sauces are the biggest headache when it comes to aircraft meals; they need to be prepared using the minimum of liquid to prevent them slopping out of the plates when served. The cabin staff was given special training in handling the menu choices. It was a great logistical feat to serve the complete eight-course menu in the 3 hours 40 minutes from Paris to New York, or 20 minutes less for departures from London.

FIRST CLASS SERVICE

"Arrive before you leave!" proclaimed the publicity, and throughout Concorde's commercial life BA and Air France targeted the "passenger in a hurry". She flew two-and-a-half times faster than a subsonic aircraft, setting standards that had to be matched by facilities on board and on the ground.

From the earliest flights to Rio de Janeiro, Air France's Concorde passengers had a special telephone contact number and their own bus service from the centre of Paris. On arrival at Charles de Gaulle Airport, porters would immediately take charge of their luggage. Checking-in took place in a reserved area, with customs formalities occupying a mere few minutes; travelers would then be directed to the Concorde lounge.

Free gifts or products on sale to Concorde passengers were equally luxurious: a model of the first operational Concorde, mono-grammed silver souvenirs and lapel pins, all of which fuelled "Concorde-mania".

THE BEST SEATS IN THE HOUSE

It was rather like the theatre—the front seats of the forward cabin were the most in demand, and you had to book well in advance to get one. Passengers mostly preferred window seats though some, including Alain Ducasse, opted to sit next the aisle where it was cooler. On Air France Concordes, rows 27 and 28 were not available; the seating was removed to make more room for luggage and to correct the aircraft's weight after the modifications to her wing tanks. BA kept these rows, but with lighter seats made of carbon and titanium upholstered in Connolly hide and dark blue fabric to a design by Terence Conran.

RIGHT & OPPOSITE
Tableware designed by the iconic Raymond Loewy's company CEI (Compagnie d'ésthétique industrielle). The cutlery was manufactured by silversmiths Bouillet-Bourdelle, the china by Raynaud of Limoges and the glassware by the Souvigny glassworks.

PAGES 110, 111
LEFT: A menu by Alain Ducasse. The famous French chef created this special meal to celebrate the millennium. The wine-list was chosen by Philippe Faure-Brac, voted world's best wine steward in 1992. At the request of a highly discerning clientele, the Faure-Brac-Ducasse partnership was maintained from December 14, 2001 to February 14, 2002. RIGHT: Seats from the forward cabin of prototype 002, 1969. This design was for customer demonstration only and was replaced on commercial models.

À l'occasion des fêtes de fin d'année, Alain Ducasse, chef de trois restaurants de haute cuisine à Monaco, Paris et New York, a imaginé pour Concorde ce menu d'exception.

Alain Ducasse, chef of three haute cuisine restaurants in Monaco, Paris and New York, has created an exceptional menu for Concorde for the Christmas and New Year's celebrations.

CHAMPAGNE

Cuvée spéciale Dom Perignon 1993

BORDEAUX BLANC LIQUOREUX

Sauternes 1ᵉʳ Grand Cru Classé 1994
Château Rieussec

BOURGOGNE BLANC

Meursault 1ᵉʳ cru 1996
Maison Labouré-Roi

BORDEAUX ROUGE

Pauillac Grand Cru Classé
Château Batailley 1996

BOURGOGNE ROUGE

Nuits-Saint-Georges 1ᵉʳ cru "Les Porêts" 1993
Maison Antonin Rodet

Les vins sont sélectionnés par Philippe Faure-Brac, meilleur sommelier du monde 1992.
The wines have been selected by the renowned 1992 world champion Wine Steward Philippe Faure-Brac.

Le Bistrot du sommelier - Paris

CAVIAR OSCIÈTRE
OSETRA CAVIAR

DÉJEUNER

CHOIX DE HORS D'ŒUVRE - CHOICE OF HORS D'ŒUVRE

Médaillons de homard breton, fondue tomatée et champignons, jus de grecque truffé
Brittany lobster medallions, tenderly reduced tomatoes and mushrooms, Greek-style truffled juice

Confit de volaille des Landes, châtaignes fondantes, truffe noire et foie gras de canard, condiment de pommes
Preserved chicken from the Landes region, tenderly cooked chestnuts, black truffle and duck foie gras, apple chutney

SALADE DE SAISON - FRESH GARDEN SALAD

Tartare de légumes et d'herbes fraîches, côtes de salades croquantes
Vegetable and fresh herb tartar with crispy salad leaves

CHOIX DE PLATS CHAUDS - CHOICE OF HOT DISHES

Filet de bar de ligne à la plancha, blanc de poireaux et céleri fondant, sauce américaine coraillée
Wild fillet of sea bass à la plancha, slowly simmered leek and celery hearts served with lobster coral sauce

Mignon de veau de lait aux champignons et truffe noire du Périgord,
légumes de saison en beaux morceaux poêlés
Veal tenderloin, mushroom and black truffle crust, roasted seasonal vegetables

Légumes gratinés aux sucs de cuisson, jeunes épinards au beurre noisette
Vegetable gratin in their cooking juice, baby spinach with browned butter

LE FROMAGE - FRENCH CHEESE

Brie de Meaux fourré de truffes noires
Brie from Meaux filled with black truffles

DUO DE DESSERTS - DESSERT DUET

Aspic d'ananas et de fruits exotiques, au parfum de citronnelle et menthe fraîche
Pineapple and exotic fruit aspic, flavoured with citronella and fresh mint

et - *and*

Croustillant choco-café au goût de moka
Crispy choco-coffee biscuit flavoured with mocha

CAFÉ THÉ LIQUEUR
COFFEE TEA BRANDIES LIQUEURS

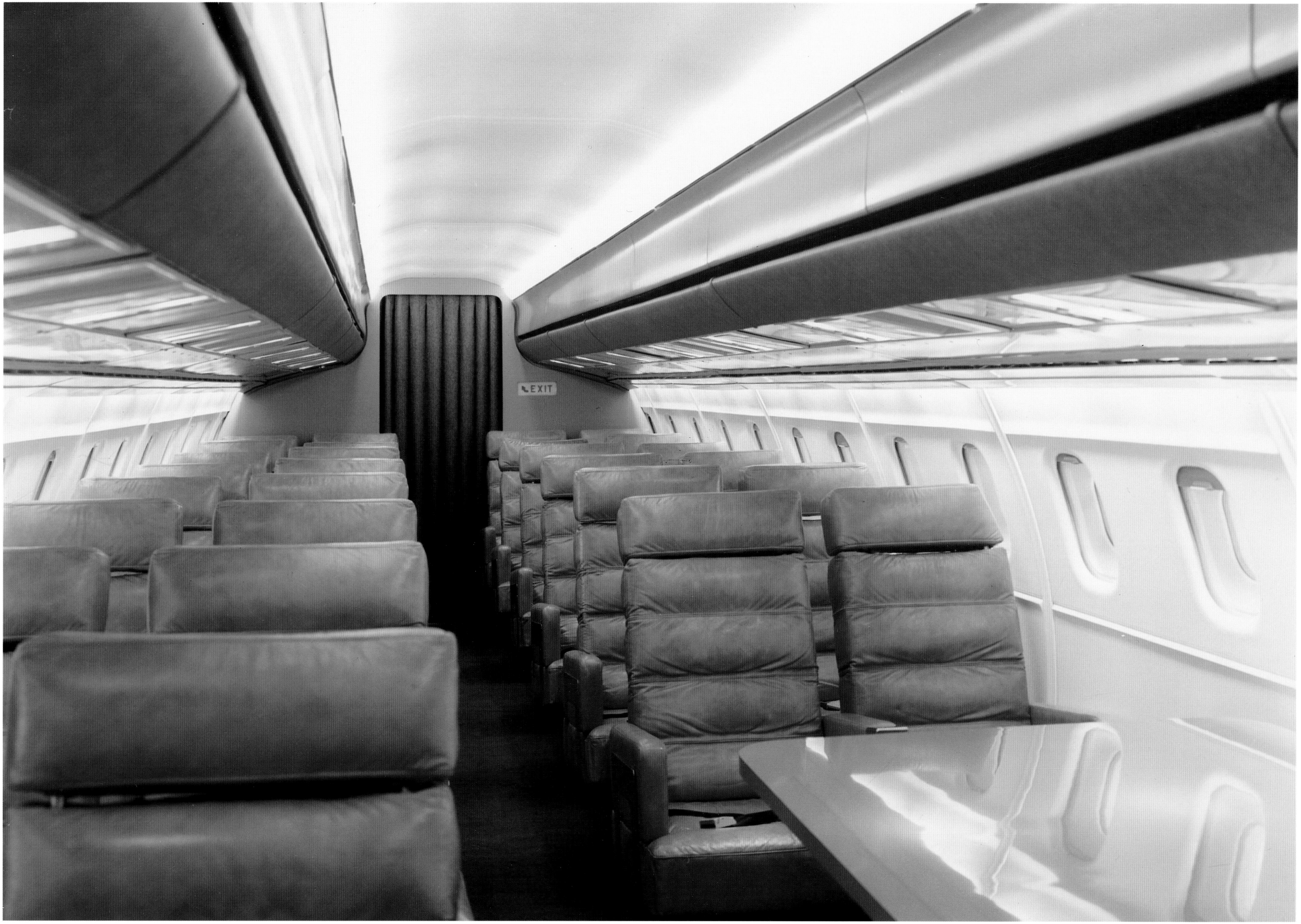
EXIT

Left Card

British airways

Issue **5**

FOR YOUR SAFETY
POUR VOTRE SÉCURITÉ
FÜR IHRE SICHERHEIT
PER LA VOSTRA SICUREZZA
PARA SU SEGURIDAD
ΓΙΑ ΤΗΝ ΑΣΦΑΛΕΙΑ ΣΑΣ

لا مانكم
आप की सुरक्षा के लिये।
آپ کی حفاظت کے لئے

安全措施
安全のしおり

Concorde

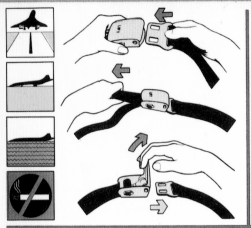

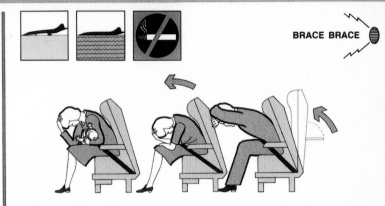

BRACE BRACE

OXYGEN

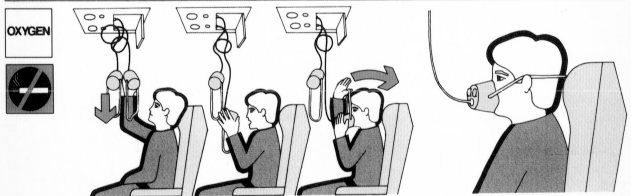

1   2   3   4

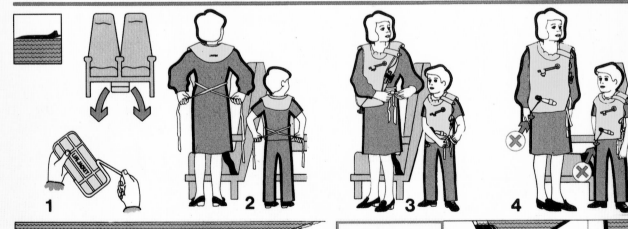

5

PSG Derby F393 (5th)

Right Card

British airways

Issue **5**

FOR YOUR SAFETY
POUR VOTRE SÉCURITÉ
FÜR IHRE SICHERHEIT
PER LA VOSTRA SICUREZZA
PARA SU SEGURIDAD
ΓΙΑ ΤΗΝ ΑΣΦΑΛΕΙΑ ΣΑΣ

لا مانكم
आप की सुरक्षा के लिये।
آپ کی حفاظت کے لئے

安全措施
安全のしおり

Concorde

   OXYGEN EXIT

Takeoff and landing	Emergency landing	Landing on water	Oxygen	Emergency exit	No smoking
Décollage et atterrissage	Atterrissage forcé	Amerrissage	Oxygène	Sortie de secours	Ne pas fumer
Start und Landung	Notlandung	Wasserung	Sauerstoff	Notausgang	Nicht rauchen
Decollo e atterraggio	Atterraggio forzato	Ammaraggio	Ossigeno	Uscita di emergenza	Non fumare
Despegue y aterrizaje	Aterrizaje forzoso	Amaraje	Oxigeno	Salida de urgencia	No fumar

起飛和降落 緊急着陸 降落水面 氧氣 太平門 禁止吸煙
離陸および着陸 緊急着陸 緊急着水 酸素 非常口 禁煙
Ἀπογείωση καί προσγείωση   Ἀναγκαστική προσγείωση   Ἀναγκαστική προσθαλάσσωση   Ὀξυγόνο   Ἔξοδος κινδύνου   Μή καπνίζετε

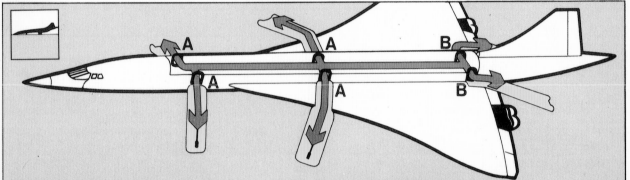

A   A   B
A   A   B

EXIT A   EXIT B

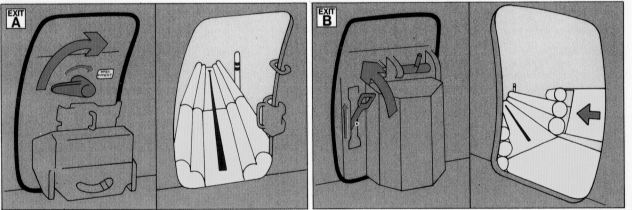

EXIT A   ✓   ✗   EXIT B

DO NOT REMOVE FROM AIRCRAFT

A JOB IN A MILLION

"Concorde pilots are not a breed apart, but a family," Air France assured its customers. The distinction was subtle but important. The company's Concorde division comprised 145 engineers and technicians to maintain the aircraft and 126 on-board personnel— 36 cockpit crew and 96 stewards and stewardesses. The numbers were slightly larger in the case of British Airways, who operated one extra aircraft.

The aspiring Concorde pilot was faced with a seriously demanding set of conditions. First, you had to wait until the company announced an internal vacancy—usually about once a year. Then you had to be in the right age-group, 55 being the limit for captains. As pilots had to retire at 60, it was clearly not in the company's interest to train someone at enormous cost for six months only to lose them in two or three years. Co-pilots were younger, on average between 40 and 50.

Candidates had to have an unblemished record over the previous five years on another type of aircraft. According to ex-fighter pilots lucky enough to have taken Concorde's controls, she was very much like the Mirage IV to fly.

OPPOSITE
Instructions for emergency procedures (BA Concorde).
RIGHT
Top couturiers were invited to design the uniforms for the cabin crew : this stewardess' outfit was created by Jean Patou (1976).

OPPOSITE
Despite the sound level reaching 89 decibels at Mach 2,
passengers experienced no discomfort. By way of comparison,
an A320 Airbus produces 79 decibels. On approach, Concorde's
sound levels dropped to 60 decibels.

LEFT
For the eighteenth anniversary of her first flight (Paris–Rio
de Janeiro), the cabins of four of the seven Concordes
were refurbished. The upholstery and interior design were
by Andrée Putman. The operation cost Air France some
830,000 euros ($1 million).

Strapped in their seats, the passengers feel a powerful acceleration. Propelled by the thrust of her four Olympus engines, Concorde rises into the air.

THREE HOURS BEFORE TAKE-OFF

Roissy-Charles-de-Gaulle Airport. Work begins three hours before take-off, which is the time needed to prepare for the flight and check the aircraft's complex systems.

The ground crew's main concern both before and during the flight is the management of the fuel. It's a real headache. With fuel tanks that contain a maximum load of 96 tonnes and an average fuel consumption of 80 to 90 tonnes on a Paris–New York flight, there is little room for maneuver should the airplane need to be re-routed. So the crew's first task is to study the weather forecast in minute detail. The flight from Paris across the Atlantic is always against prevailing winds, which increases fuel consumption, as does air temperature: the hotter the air the aircraft encounters, the more fuel it uses. "Everything's stretched to the very limit," explains a flight engineer. "The slightest problem means we have to change route and land at a back-up airport." In any case, filling Concorde's fuel tanks takes time. If it is done too quickly, the airplane tends to tilt nose up, causing fuel to flow to the rear tanks. After fueling, many calculations need to be done, to determine speed during the different phases of the journey and to configure the engines according to wind, temperature and atmospheric pressure.

ONE HOUR THIRTY MINUTES BEFORE TAKE-OFF

One hour and thirty minutes before take-off the flight crew comes aboard. There are nearly 200 dials, indicators and warning lights on Concorde. The essential circuits, about a hundred in all, have to be tested one by one. Check-lists are long and meticulous. Concorde is a sensitive aircraft and warning signals and minor faults are a daily feature of the pilots' lives. The computers give them problems too. Flight crew and mechanics then engage in long discussions, or rather "negotiations", over the technical restrictions imposed by the regulations.

While all this is going on, the passengers are calmly boarding the aircraft. The engines start up. To save fuel Concorde must get to her runway as quickly as possible. Even though the airliner is given a certain priority over other airplanes, she takes an average of ten to fifteen minutes to taxi into position. In the cockpit, the flight engineer keeps his eyes fixed on the temperature of the brakes. He is worried they might catch fire. Even at low speed, the jet engines are liable to produce too much thrust, so the brakes need to be permanently applied. Concorde is about to take off. Her nose is lowered by 5 degrees. We're away! The captain pushes the four throttle levers and ignites the afterburner.

This system increases thrust by injecting fuel into the hot gases of the engines, so producing 25 per cent more power. In less than thirty seconds the aircraft goes from 0 to 230 mph (370 kmh). The pilots and the flight engineer keep a close eye on the engines, particularly the afterburner. If it is not functioning before a speed of 70 mph (110 kmh) is reached, the take-off is aborted.

READY FOR TAKE-OFF

Strapped in their seats, the passengers feel a powerful acceleration. Propelled by the thrust of her four Olympus engines, Concorde rises into the air. The afterburner is soon cut out to conform with anti-noise regulations over urban areas. Her nose is raised in line with the fuselage. Less than fifteen minutes after take-off the airliner is flying over Le Havre at about 29,500 ft (9,000 m). Concorde heads out to sea. The afterburner is turned back on. The machmeter rapidly rises: 0.97 … 0.98 … 0.99. The all-important moment has come. Concorde reaches Mach 1, the speed of sound. And nothing happens … much to the disappointment of some of the passengers. No shudder, no sonic bang audible inside the aircraft. Some passengers applaud. This acceleration tends to alter the balance between the centre of lift and the

centre of gravity, causing Concorde to go nose down. To counter this, the flight engineer has to alter the balance between the different fuel tanks. He immediately transfers 10 tonnes of fuel from the front to the rear of the aircraft. This re-distribution of weight is maintained all the time Concorde is flying at supersonic speeds. The airliner continues to accelerate and climb as her fuel load decreases. An hour after take-off she exceeds Mach 2. She is flying as fast as a rifle bullet.

LIKE A FIGHTER PLANE

The crew has a whole host of dials to monitor. Concorde's highly accurate, complex and sensitive systems mean she has to be piloted like a fighter plane, keeping the crew on their toes constantly. As soon as one parameter changes, others change too. Concorde cruises at an altitude of between 50,000 and 60,000 ft (15,000 to 18,000 m). She is now over Newfoundland. At Mach 2 skin friction is considerable and the nose cone of the airplane heats up to as much as 260 °F (127 °C). The temperature of the outer "skin" exceeds 194°F (90 °C) and the windows become very hot to the touch, though the air temperature outside ranges from –58 °F to –76 °F (–50 °C to –60°C). Determined by the speed of the airplane and the outside temperature, the

PAGES 116, 117
Concorde's itinerary. Three routes have been specially reserved for her over the North Atlantic. The outward route is called "Sierra Mike", the return one "Sierra Oscar". There is also a diversionary route. Whereas winds are a crucial factor in determining the itinerary of subsonic aircraft, they do not affect Concorde's. She flies well above atmospheric disturbances. This air map, used by the pilots as a flight plan, is known as a "track".

OPPOSITE
Concorde on her "launch pad". Two hours before take-off, the in-flight meals are brought on board. They will soon be followed by a hundred or so passengers who will disembark in New York just four hours later. Concorde reduces the transatlantic journey time by an impressive amount—a 10.30 departure from Europe gets into JFK, New York at 8.00—an ideal time for businessmen. However, due to the difference in international time zones, a departure at 8.00 from New York in the opposite direction means arrival in London or Paris at around 17.00.

New York has welcomed Concorde for more than twenty years and it's with immense pride that New Yorkers greet the return of this symbol of trade between Europe and the United States. Welcome home, Concorde. RUDOLPH GIULIANI, MAYOR OF NEW YORK, NOVEMBER 2002, WHEN FLIGHTS RESUMED

temperature of the aircraft's outer skin therefore needs constant monitoring. If the air temperature outside increases, the engines' speed can be reduced to prevent overheating, and vice versa.

Another, rather unexpected physical change takes place when Concorde is in flight. When on the ground she measures 202 ft 4 ins (61.66 m) in length, but when flying at 59,000 ft (18,000 m), she grows by nearly 6 in (15 cm). The passengers in their cabin remain blissfully unaware. They are happily drinking well-cooled champagne, savoring delicious food, and enjoying the remarkably smooth journey. Concorde is cruising far above the height at which conventional jet aircraft operate and so is not afflicted by the air turbulence found at lower altitudes.

DESCENT INTO NEW YORK

Through the small cabin windows, the sky is midnight blue. After flying for about two hours, and now just thirty minutes from the American coast, it is time to prepare to land at JFK, New York. The descent is almost as quick as the take-off. Throttle back, final use of two thrust reversers, back into subsonic flight to accelerate the descent and transfer the remaining fuel, this time to the front of

the aircraft. In a few minutes Concorde is once more flying below the speed of sound. The effect of the decrease in speed soon shows up on the fuel gauge. The slower the airliner travels, the more fuel she consumes, having been designed to maximize fuel efficiency at Mach 2. During the descent, the passenger cabin and cockpit can both become extremely hot. However, the fuel in the tanks remains relatively cool and so can be circulated to act as a coolant. If Concorde has been too thirsty during the flight, there could be no more than 15 tonnes of fuel left in the tanks. Consequently, the temperature in the cockpit and cabin could climb to over 95 °F (35 °C). Radio contact with JFK is established. The drooping nose is lowered by 12.5 degrees and the outer windshield retracted to give the crew a better view of what is ahead. Tension in the cockpit goes up a notch prior to the final approach and landing. Concorde presents a problem for air traffic controllers. As she gets close to JFK Airport, she once again finds herself in an "aerial traffic jam", but, as at take-off she is given priority over other aircraft, which are moved aside to allow her through. Because she is delta-winged, she makes a quick descent. She has to adopt a nose-up attitude to give her wings the best

lift at lower speeds. Her approach speed is about 190 mph (300 kmh), compared with a Boeing 747's 160 mph (257 kmh). Paradoxically, the slower she flies, the harder her engines have to work and the more noise she makes. The landing gear slips into position, the runway is in sight. Concorde lands, having crossed the Atlantic in less than four hours. Welcome to New York!

OPPOSITE
At take-off, thanks to the afterburner, the thrust/weight ratio is one and a half times greater than that of a Boeing 747. This is why it takes Concorde less time to leave the ground. When the brakes are released, Concorde only needs eight seconds to reach 62 mph (100 kmh).

PAGES 122, 123
LEFT & RIGHT: The afterburner is used at take-off but the pilot cuts it out after thirty seconds. When this happens, the passengers feel a slight braking sensation. At night the afterburner is clearly visible.

121

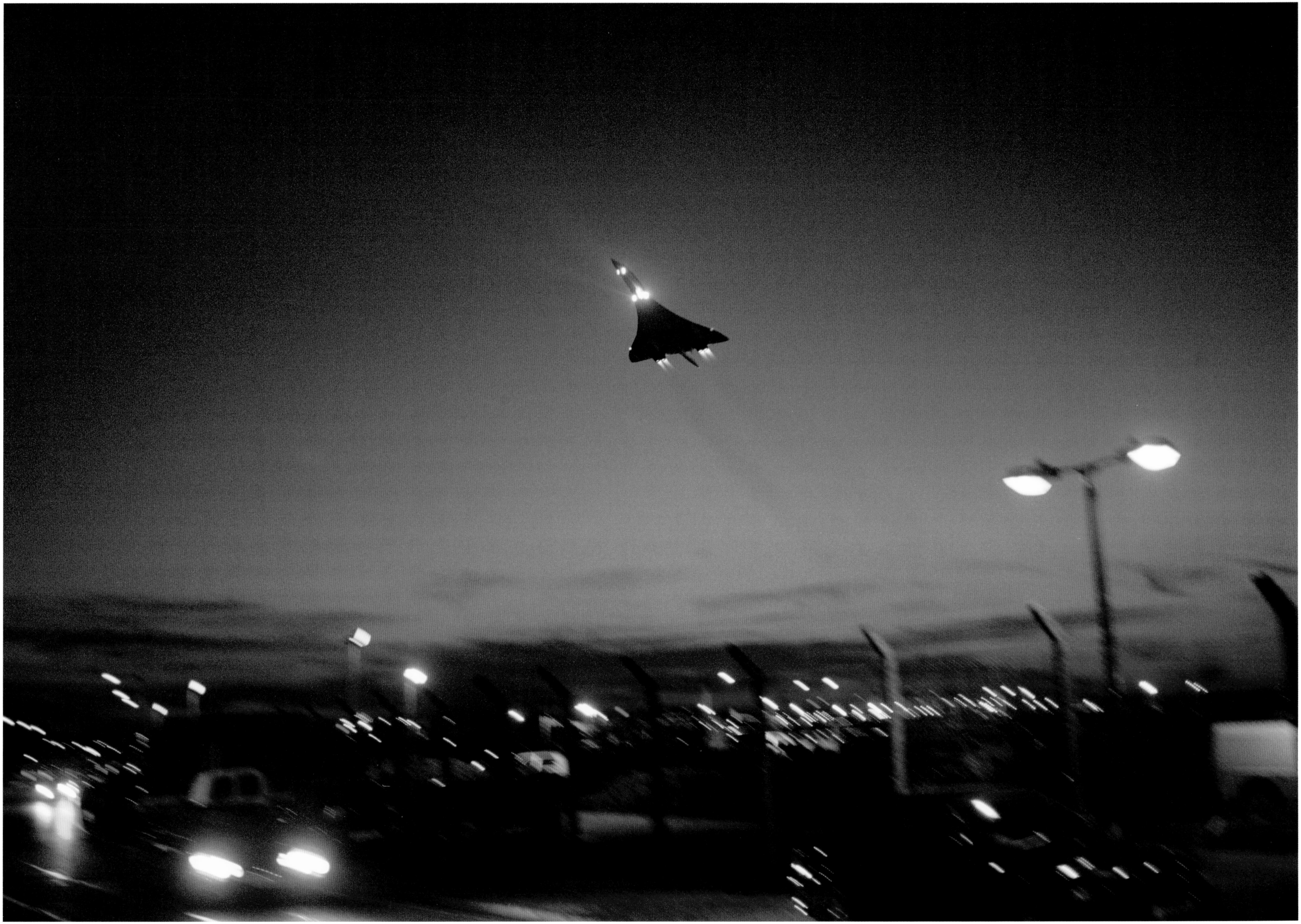

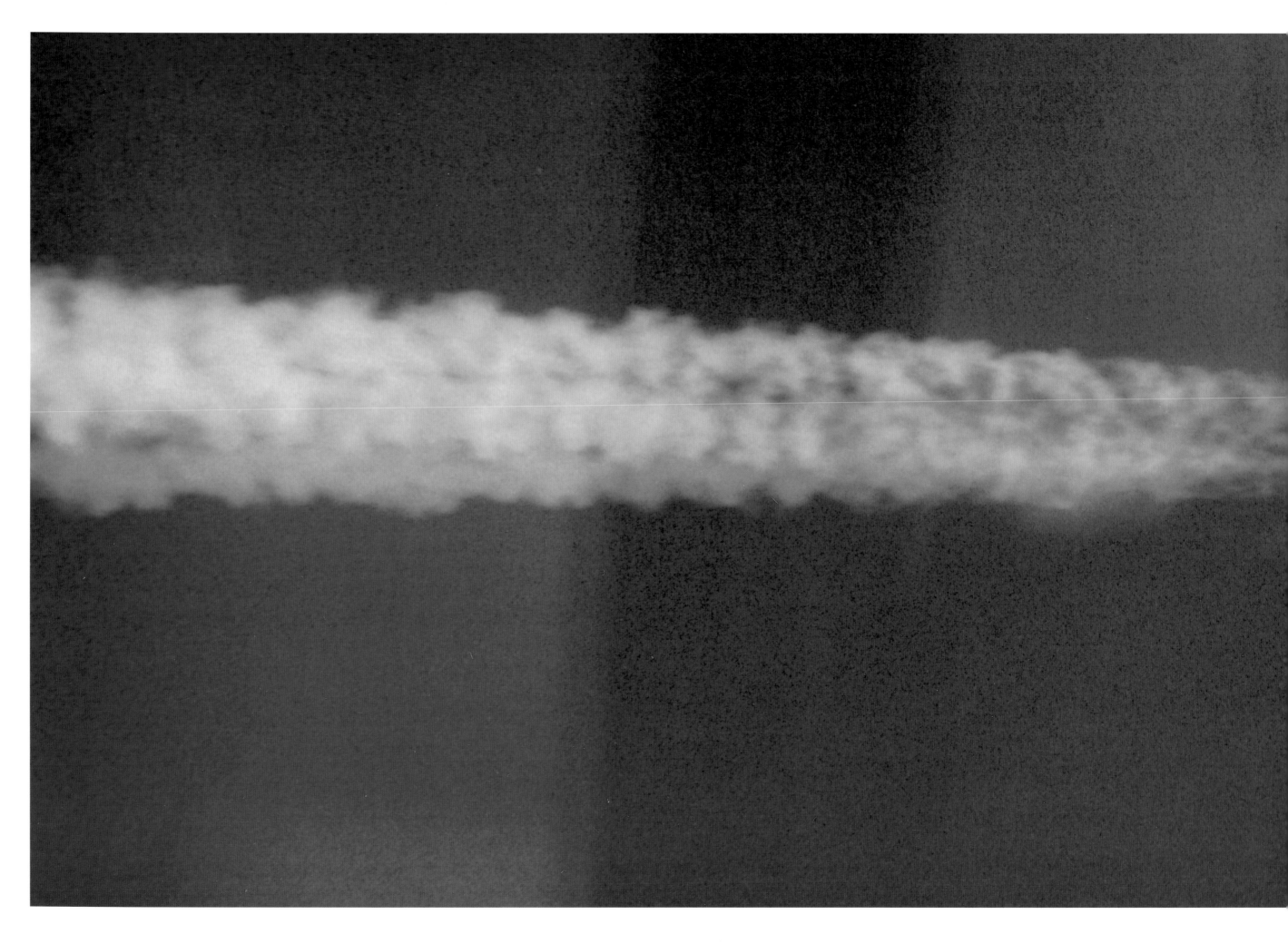

The aircraft is only allowed to break through the sound barrier over the sea or desert, to avoid disturbing any inhabitants below. After leaving Europe, pilots must maintain a level course at a subsonic speed (Mach 0.93) and an average altitude of about 29,500 ft (9,000 m) until they are over the Atlantic. Then Concorde can accelerate and climb rapidly to reach its cruising speed and altitude.

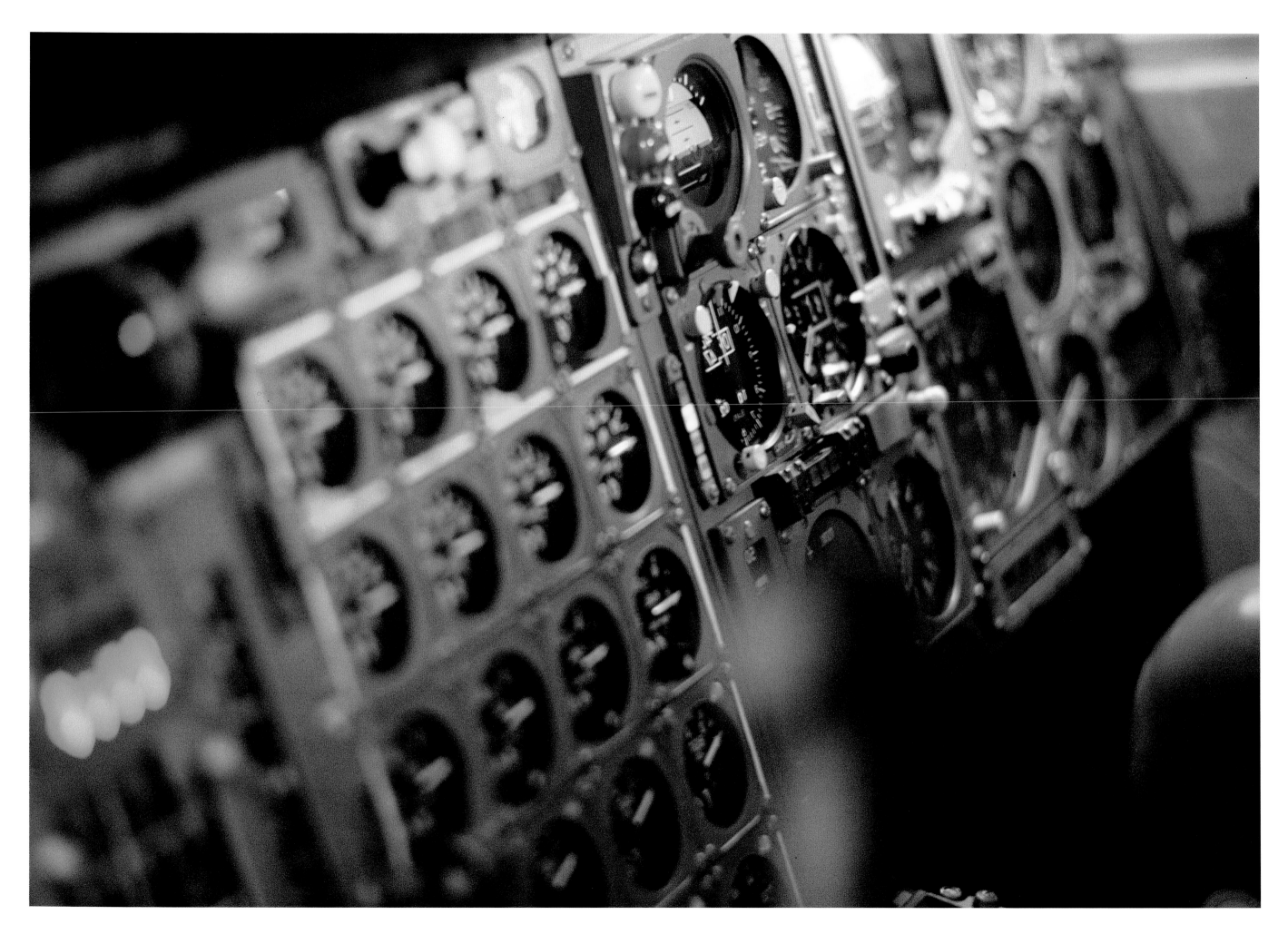

OPPOSITE
A profusion of dials, indicator lights and switches. There
are more than 200 in all. The cockpit was designed at the
beginning of the 1960s. Today its analog instrument panels
look totally out-of-date, betraying the airliner's true age.
LEFT
Mach 2.01, just over 1,320 mph (2,124 kmh): this is Concorde's
supersonic cruising speed. The aircraft is then flying at twice
the speed of sound. During the flight, the machmeter reveals
some slight variations, since the Mach number is a relative
speed (the ratio of the aircraft's speed to the speed of sound
in the surrounding atmosphere).

THIRTY YEARS OF TECHNOLOGICAL SPIN-OFFS

"What's the latest on Concorde?" How many times did French president General de Gaulle open cabinet meetings in the 1960s with this question, indicating just how big the stakes were. There may have been a gap of fifteen years between the very first designs and the first commercial flights, but this was because Concorde's complicated systems had extremely demanding requirements, necessitating a whole host of technological innovations. The technological advances made as a result enabled the European aircraft manufacturer Airbus to offer a range of aircraft with electronic control systems similar to those used in Concorde. They were used on the A320 during the late 1980s. This gave Airbus a big advantage over Boeing, whose pilots had to undertake a two-month training course to transfer, for example, from 737s to 777s. The side stick, similar to a computer joystick, was also tested on one of the Concorde prototypes.

The fuel transfer system, operated by the flight engineer, was another crucial step forward for the aeronautical industry. As the aircraft's weight acted downwards at the centre of gravity and its lift acted upwards at the centre of lift, with thirty or so pumps drawing fuel from Concorde's sixteen tanks, the transfer of fuel shifted the aircraft's centre of gravity back by about 5 ft (1.5 m) to align it with the centre of lift, which moved aft during the transition from subsonic to supersonic flight. This enabled the aircraft to be kept stable. Otherwise the controls would have had to be kept deflected, causing excessive drag. It would have been like accelerating while keeping one foot on the brake. This technique, which had already been used on Marcel Dassault's Mirage 4 bomber, has been further developed on most civil aircraft over the last decade. The transfers are now done automatically and enable enormous quantities of fuel to be saved.

Besides fueling the engines and performing the role of mobile ballast, the fuel has a third function, that of coolant. When Concorde was at cruising altitude, the outside air temperature was close to –67 °F (–56 °C) and her fuselage heated up due to skin friction. Circulating in a heat exchanger, fuel was used to cool the air in the cabin, the jet engine fittings and all heat-sensitive equipment. The problems experienced with high temperature gave rise to further research, benefiting many areas far removed from aeronautics. The Teflon used on frying pans and saucepans was originally developed for flight control shafts. Adhesives and composite materials with a base of fiberglass or carbon are now used on yachts and in the automotive industry. The light alloy AU2GN that tolerates 312 °F (150 °C), the special kinds of steel used for the landing gear, titanium, heat-resistant nickel and cobalt, all required the development of specialized metallurgy. The first computerized machine tools for milling large metal sheets were introduced in France to help build Concorde. Braking was another area of research. During an emergency stop to abort take-off, the 185-tonne aircraft, moving at nearly 250 mph (400 kmh), had less than 6,560 ft (2,000 m) in which to come to a halt. Only carbon discs, which can resist temperatures of 2,500 °F (1,200 °C), were found to be capable of producing such braking power when combined with an anti-skid device, which subsequently led to the development of the now ubiquitous ABS (Antilock Braking System) used in cars. The fact that braking is easier to control on both modern airplanes and automobiles is largely due to Concorde.

Concorde taxiing towards the take-off runway. The delta wing is the structure most suited to supersonic flight. Behind the exhaust nozzles, the eyelid-shaped thrust reversers can be seen. They are used to reduce speed rapidly during flight or landing.

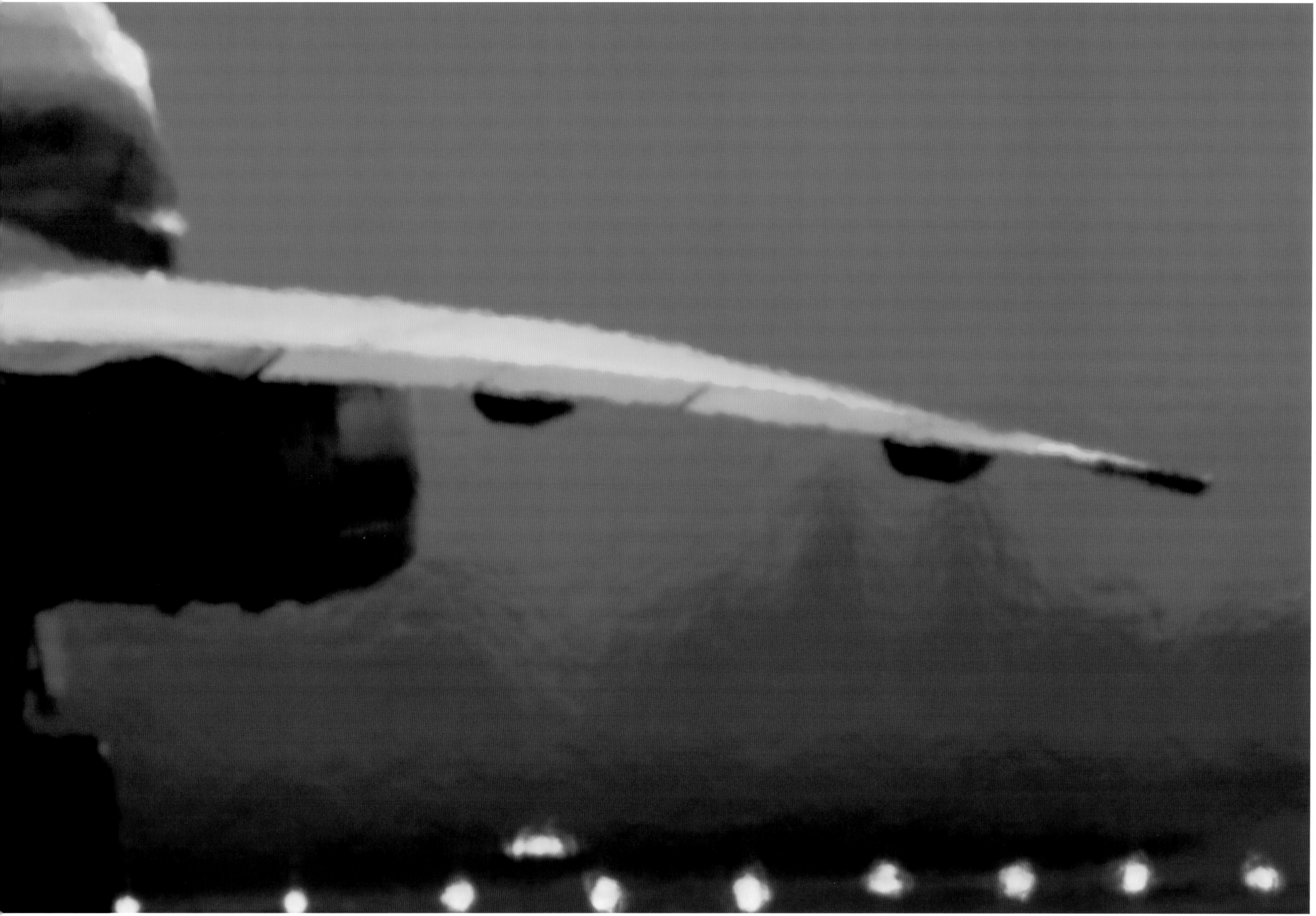

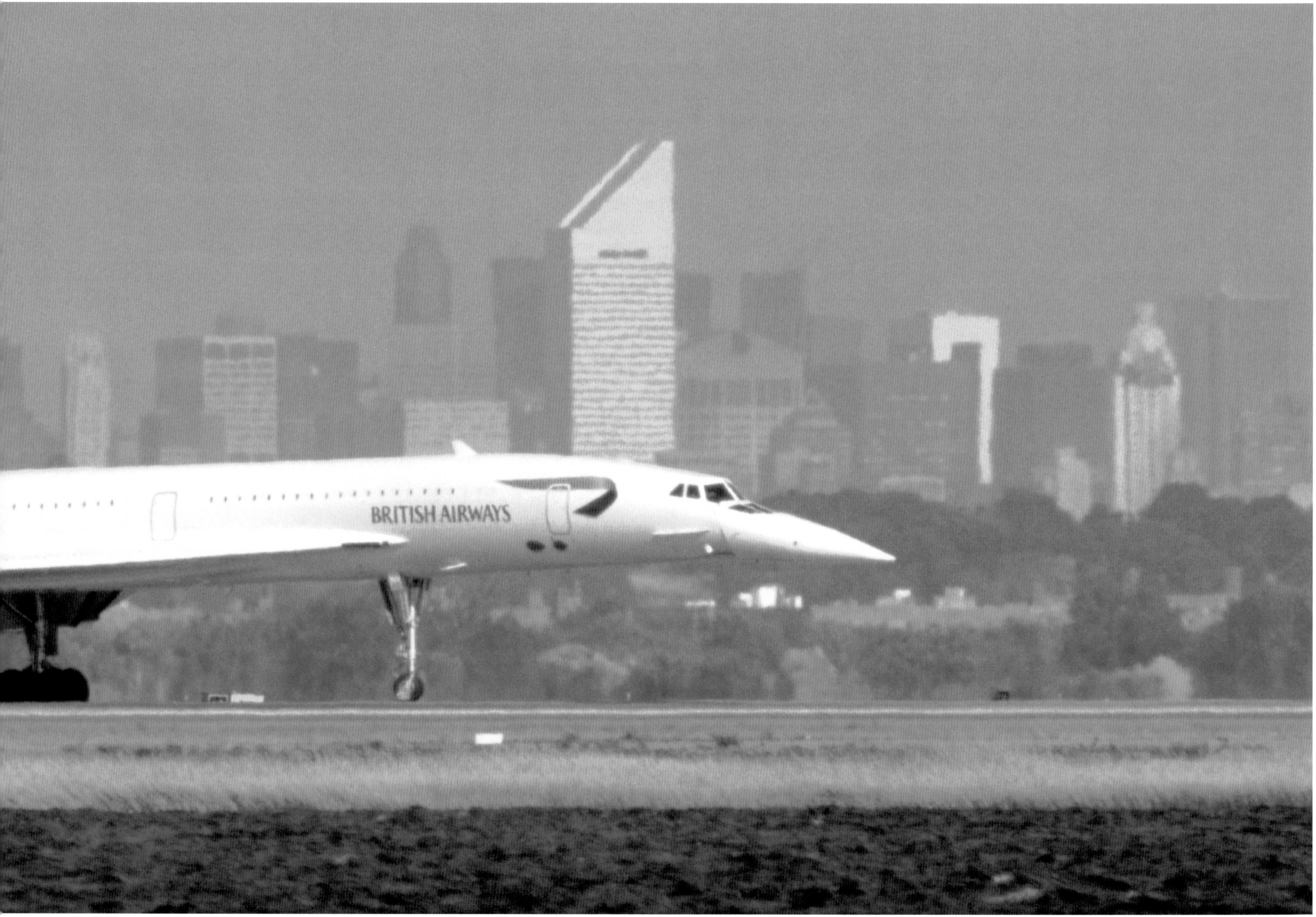
BRITISH AIRWAYS

PAGES 130, 131
A rare shot of a British Airways Concorde G-BOAC taking off on runway 22, left, at JFK Airport, New York. The airliner did not often use this runway because of American anti-noise regulations. However, on this particular day, September 12, 2003, it was allowed to take off towards the south-west, because of a strong cross wind on runway 31. In the background are the skyscrapers of Manhattan, including on the extreme left, the Chrysler Building.

RIGHT
Concorde has just landed on runway 27 at Roissy after a 3 hour 45 minute flight from New York. The flight time between London and New York is five minutes less than the Paris–New York trip.
OPPOSITE
The pilot applies maximum thrust. At take-off Concorde's nose is lowered by 5 degrees and its visor retracted. The high ambient humidity makes it seem as if there is a halo around the aircraft. This is caused by swirls of condensation, also known as vortices.

IN THE HANGAR

PAGES 134, 135
Concorde "dozing" at Roissy, waiting for the first take-off
of the day.
LEFT
Air France's maintenance hangars. Due to her complexity,
Concorde demanded the most meticulous attention, requiring
almost eighteen hours of maintenance for every hour in flight.
In comparison, a Boeing 747 requires just a little less than
two hours and an Airbus one hour ten minutes.

ETERNAL YOUTH?

Concorde airliners still look fairly new due to the relatively few hours that they spent in the air in comparison with other civil aircraft. In twenty-seven years of operation, very few British Airways or Air France Concordes flew more than 20,000 hours each, whereas subsonic long-haul aircraft generally reach this figure in just five or six years. In 1976, the year in which she came into operation, Concorde only flew an average of 3 hours 15 minutes a day and as a result she did not suffer significantly from corrosion. Flying "above the weather" and being hangared more frequently than other aircraft when not in use, also helped preserve her appearance. Concorde remained so "youthful" that in 1999, the year of her thirtieth anniversary, Air France was even planning to extend the life of its fleet by around ten years. But though technically very advanced for her era and still unequalled in performance, Concorde is now clearly technologically obsolete.

HIGH-PRECISION ENGINEERING

Because of her complexity, Concorde required a very high level of maintenance. Since all her systems involved complicated electronics, they required the use of computers to process all the data. Engineers and technicians trying to detect faults were faced, therefore, with real difficulties. As a result, there were long periods when the aircraft was out of operation and subject to meticulous inspections: eighteen hours of maintenance for just one hour of flight. At Air France it took a team of 120 engineers and technicians to maintain the aircraft. The four Rolls-Royce SNECMA Olympus 593 Mk. 610 engines demanded particular attention, since this was where faults were more likely to occur.

The problems associated with supersonic flight at Mach 2 frequently led to multiple faults in the distribution systems for lubricants and in the high pressure pumps. Likewise, variable geometry air inlet valves needed very careful monitoring in order to avoid flooding. But that was not all. As already discussed, at speeds of Mach 2 the nose cone heated up due to skin friction and could reach temperatures of 260 °F (127 °C). The fuselage expanded and Concorde grew by 6 inches (15 cm) in length. All of which resulted in maintenance costs that were three times greater than those for a subsonic long-haul jet. In 1986, Air France took stock. In ten years, Concorde had flown more than 45,000 hours and carried 620,000 passengers. Each aircraft had averaged 1,900 take-off and landing cycles, but the lifespan of the airplane was estimated to be 6,700 cycles. Logically, Concorde had many more days of service ahead of her. British Airways and Air France even entered into discussions with the manufacturers about extending the aircraft's working life to 8,500 cycles, thereby allowing the fleet to continue in service until 2006. But the accident at Gonesse in July 2000 and the terrorist attacks of September 11, 2001, were to shatter these plans totally.

EXHAUSTIVE INSPECTIONS

The construction consortium had devised a very detailed servicing and maintenance program for the aircraft. Before each flight, as part of a routine daily check, Concorde's mechanics inspected the fuselage, wheels, landing gear and engines. During the five hours before departure, the flight mechanic and an expert ground staff technician then inspected and verified all the electrical circuits, the command functions, and all the instruments and the security systems. After a total of 210 flying hours, a first detailed check called the "A" check took place, followed by, at 420 hours, the "B" check.

When an aircraft reached 1,624 flying hours, it was grounded for a week's inspection, known as the "C" check. Then, after 6,000 hours, came the "lay-over" or intermediate inspection, which represented three months of testing in the maintenance hangar, involving some 12,000 man-hours. The mechanics carried out many different levels of tests, replacing every component that might be faulty.

Eventually, after 12,000 flying hours, it was time for a major overhaul. In September 1989, the oldest of the Air France Concordes, F-BVFA, which had entered service on January 21, 1976, became the first of the company's six aircraft to be subjected to this exhaustive inspection. After flying 11,650 hours and traveling 20 million kilometers (12.5 million miles), F-BVFA was stripped and dismantled piece by piece leaving only the basic framework. Every component was analyzed and x-rayed in search of the smallest fault. This huge project took eleven months and involved 40,000 man-hours. After F-BVFA, her sister aircraft F-BVFB underwent the same treatment, in April 1996, followed by F-BVFC and F-BTSC in April 1998.

OPPOSITE
Each full inspection takes a year on average. The aircraft is dismantled piece by piece. The fuselage, the wings and the fin are inspected, either visually or by X-ray, to detect the slightest weakness. Above, the tail-pipe of the two prototypes, 001 and 002.

PAGES 140, 141
RIGHT & LEFT: F-BVFA gets ready for her new life. The full inspection of this series 5 Concorde took 40,000 man-hours.

The bodywork was stripped at Orly, and then painted in khaki-colored anti-corrosion paint at Roissy. Everything was X-rayed: not a single square inch escaped inspection.

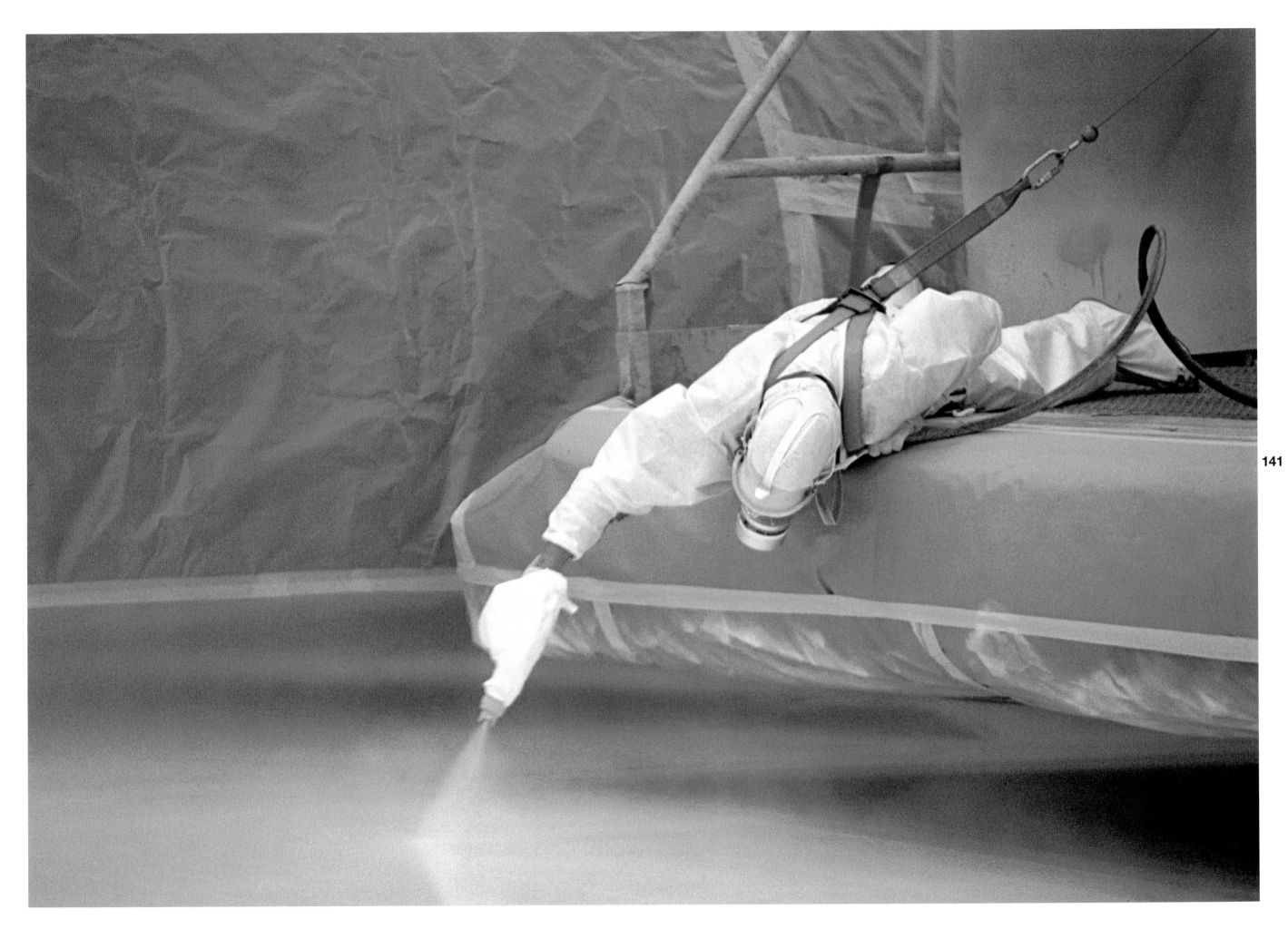

CONCORDE:
PRINCIPAL FEATURES

Length: 204 ft (62.10 m)

Wingspan: 84 ft (25.55 m)

Height (ground to top of fin): 38 ft (11.40 m)

Width of fuselage: 9 ft 5 in (2.87 m)

Wing surface: 3,856 sq ft (358.22 sq m)

Take-off distance: 3,500 yds (3,200 m)

Landing distance: 2,670 yds (2,440 m)

Maximum speed: Mach 2.23 (approx. 1472 mph/ 2368 kmh)

Cruising speed: Mach 2.02 (approx. 1,350 mph/ 2,179 kmh)

Average landing speed: 185 mph (260 kmh)

Minimum speed: 137 mph (221 kmh)

Operational altitude: 59,000 ft (18,300 m)

Maximum altitude: 65,000 ft (20,025 m)

Maximum range: 4,100 miles (6,500 km) (100 passengers)

Propulsion: 4 Rolls-Royce SNECMA Olympus 593 engines

Thrust: 4 x 38,000 lbs, i.e. a total of 152,000 lbs

Weight empty: 170,000 lbs (77,500 kg)

Maximum weight at take-off: 408,000 lbs (185,070 kg)

Maximum fuel: 211,600 lbs (96,000 kg)

Maximum payload: 27,900 lbs (12,700 kg)

Maximum fuel consumption (afterburner): 87 tonnes per hour

Fuel tank capacity: 30,976 US gallons (117,285 liters) plus 21.13 US gallons (80 liters) of oil

Fuel consumption at take-off: 13 tonnes during the first twenty-three minutes of flight

Consumption during flight: 18 tonnes per hour

Consumption per passenger New York–Paris: 20.4 miles per US gallon (7.23 km per liter)

Concorde's maintenance costs were on average ten times higher than those of a subsonic aircraft and accounted for more than 40 per cent of her operating costs. When cruising at supersonic speeds the fuselage heated up, resulting in a temperature at the front of the airplane that sometimes reached 260°F (127°C). However, this also had the effect of limiting corrosion, a major cause of ageing in subsonic aircraft.

144

RIGHT
Before and after every flight, the engines, considered the most
vulnerable part of the aircraft, were inspected meticulously.
OPPOSITE
After the accident at Gonesse in July 2000, flexible Kevlar
protective linings were installed inside the fuel tanks of
Air France and British Airways Concordes. This was to limit
any leaks that might have occurred under the wing, should
its structure be damaged. Small perforations were made in
these linings to enable small amounts of fuel to continue
to circulate and cool the "skin" of the aircraft to prevent
overheating during supersonic flight.

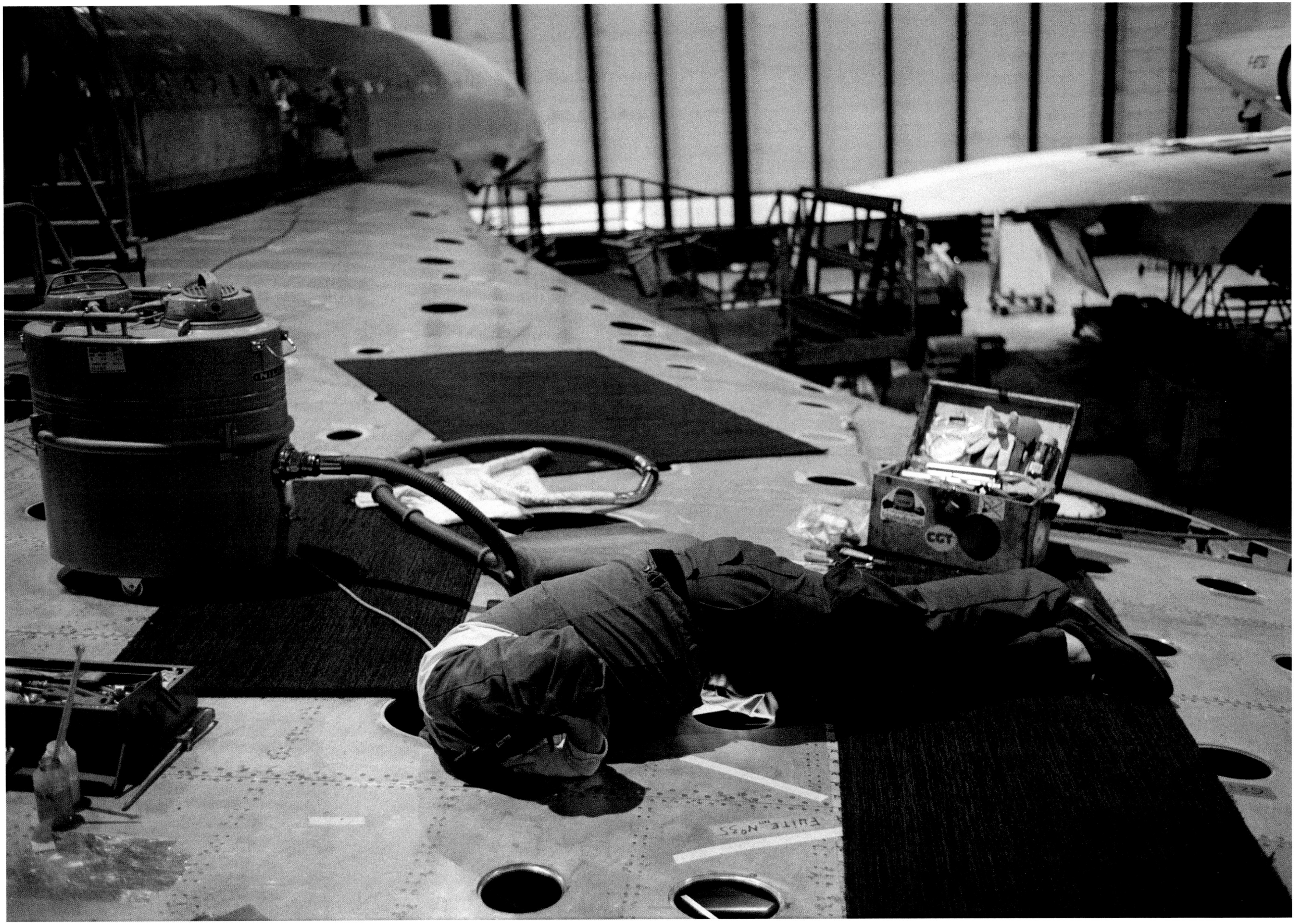
CGT

RIGHT
When removed from the aircraft, the Olympus engine's fuel pipe is plugged to prevent fuel from leaking during transportation.
OPPOSITE
F-WTSA gets a spring-clean. This is Concorde 102, the second pre-series aircraft. Her career was very short: forty months of flight trials and only 656 hours in the air. She landed for the last time at Orly Airport on May 20, 1976. After several years of neglect, she was saved by volunteers from the Delta Museum at Athis-Mons, south of Orly.
PAGES 148, 149
LEFT: Concorde has a shower. Once a year each aircraft was cleaned with jets of water.
RIGHT: Paris–New York or London–New York. Less than 3 hours 30 minutes to cover 3,530 miles (5,700 kms), including 1 hour 40 minutes at Mach 2 at an altitude of 50,000–60,000 ft (15,000–18,000 m).

WARNING
DO NOT
PRESSURISE

TRANSPORT
BLANK
ONLY

147

LEFT

It is night-time at Roissy and Concorde has just landed. An Air France employee inspects the aircraft. At low speeds she has a very high angle of attack, which explains the tail wheel. When landing or taking off, the airliner is nose-up and her aft sometimes touches the ground.

OPPOSITE

Close-up of the shock absorber on the landing gear. After October 2000, a new Michelin radial tire called the NZG (Near Zero Growth) became available. Because it expanded very little, it had the advantage of fragmenting rather than bursting if damaged.

PAGES 152, 153

LEFT: The Rolls-Royce Olympus 593 MK 610 jet engine produced a thrust of 38,000 lbs.

RIGHT: Rear view of the Olympus jet engine. The stainless steel "eyelids" with their honeycomb structure were manufactured by SNECMA.

THE BIRTH OF
A LEGEND

> *Concorde has been underestimated.*
> *In time we will understand what a step forward it was...*

MSTISLAV ROSTROPOVITCH, CELLIST AND CONDUCTOR

INTO RETIREMENT

Following the accident at Gonesse involving an Air France Concorde on July 25, 2000, shortly after take off from Roissy, the Anglo-French aircraft was on borrowed time. She was withdrawn from service when her certificate of airworthiness, her license to fly, was suspended a few days after the accident. Aircraft had only been withdrawn from service twice before in aviation history: the DC-10 was grounded in 1987 following an accident in the United States, and Comet 1 was withdrawn in 1954 after two had crashed and was never returned to service. The many modifications made to Concorde following the tragic accident and the resumption of commercial flights on November 7, 2001, changed nothing and though she returned to service briefly it proved to be largely symbolic. She regained her certificate of airworthiness on September 5, 2001. But just a few days later, on September 11, four aircraft belonging to United Airlines and American Airlines were hijacked and crashed into the Twin Towers of the World Trade Center in Manhattan, the Pentagon in the Washington suburbs and into the ground near Pittsburgh, Pennsylvania. The accident at Gonesse, combined with the effects of the terrorist attacks on 9/11 and the war in Iraq,

had sounded the airliner's death knell. The devastating attacks in America further caused a collapse of air traffic worldwide. The decision by Air France and British Airways to resume flights to New York, taken on November 7, 2001, was designed above all to reassure. "We hope that the resumption of Concorde flights will mark a return of confidence to New York and confirm there is still a strong demand for air travel between Great Britain and the United States," declared Rod Eddington, chief executive of British Airways. Jean-Cyril Spinetta, president of Air France, saw it as a tribute to the inhabitants of a city still reeling from the recent terrorist attacks. "We at Air France haven't forgotten the expressions of sympathy and support from the people of New York in the hours and days after the accident on July 25, 2000." But the public's confidence was no longer there.

Very soon, the proportion of seats being filled fell below 50 per cent of total capacity. At the same time, Air France and British Airways were confronted with a dramatic increase in maintenance costs. The outbreak of the Iraq war in early 2003 only made the situation worse. Air France and British Airways were left in no doubt: it was high time to put an end to these costs.

MAY 31, 2003, 17:45

On April 10, 2003, the two companies simultaneously announced the withdrawal of Concorde after twenty-seven years of commercial operation.

The chief executives of Air France and British Airways had little choice: the decision to put an end to Concorde's career came indirectly from EADS, the European Aeronautic Defense and Space Company, who no longer wanted, through its Airbus division, to meet the airliner's investment and maintenance costs. The last Air France flight took place on May 31, 2003. On that day, at 17:45, flight AF 001 from New York landed for the last time on the tarmac at Roissy-Charles-de-Gaulle. British Airways, who had been filling more seats than Air France and had a larger stock of spare parts, continued operating Concorde for a few more months, until October 24, 2003. The pilot on the last New York–London flight was Mike Bannister, who had joined the Concorde team in 1977 as the youngest pilot in the fleet. Throughout the autumn of 2003, Concorde said farewell to Great Britain. During the last week of commercial operations, a Concorde left Heathrow every day to carry out a low-level subsonic fly-past over a different British city. On board were many guests of British Airways and members

PAGES 154, 155
An illustration based on a poster created in 1983 by Raymond Moretti to mark the fiftieth anniversary of Air France. The artist commented, "I drew line after line until I triggered in myself an impression of vibrations, heat, cold, infinity...."

OPPOSITE
French plane spotter, Jean Dieuzaide, and the famous photographer Robert Doisneau (on the right in the photograph), watch as Concorde's jet engines are put through their paces on the runways of Sud Aviation.

PAGES 160, 161

LEFT: After her final landing at JFK Airport, British Airways Concorde G-BOAD is transported on a 250 ft (80 m) barge to the Intrepid Sea, Air and Space Museum on the banks of the Hudson River, where she was placed beside the aircraft carrier *Intrepid*.

RIGHT: New York, 1997: to mark Thanksgiving Day British Airways exhibits a model of Concorde in its new livery.

LEFT:

Concorde is transported along the Thames past the Houses of Parliament, where, forty years earlier, British MPs had decided to join forces with the French to produce a supersonic passenger aircraft.

Concorde, a beautiful bird! A magnificent aircraft no longer in the sky, but always in our minds. GERARD DEPARDIEU, ACTOR

of the public who had won their places in a lottery. On October 20, Concorde flew over Birmingham, on the 21st Belfast, the 22nd Manchester, the 23rd Cardiff and finally, on October 24, three Concordes flew in from Edinburgh, New York and from a round trip over the Bay of Biscay, to make their final landings at Heathrow.

On the eve of its final withdrawal, the Queen allowed Windsor Castle to be illuminated as Concorde flew overhead: a supreme honor usually reserved for major heads of state.

BRANSON FLIES TO CONCORDE'S RESCUE

A billionaire's whim or just another publicity stunt? As soon as her withdrawal from service was announced, Richard Branson, never long out of the media spotlight, tried to buy a British Airways Concorde for the sum of… one pound sterling ($1.75). The Virgin Atlantic boss's offer was based on a legal point arising from the contract between the British government and British Airways.

Branson claimed that in 1987, when British Airways was privatized, the government sold seven Concorde airplanes to the company at the symbolic price of £1. The contract stipulated that, should British Airways fail, another operator could be authorized to fly the aircraft. Writing in *The Economist* magazine on October 23, 2003, Branson raised the bid to £5 million (approximately $9 million) but had to abandon his plan when faced with a categorical refusal from British Airways' management.

A MUSEUM PIECE

Should Concorde have been saved? Opinions are still divided, even today. Putting economic considerations aside, Concorde is still the embodiment of a dream and is one of the aeronautical industry's finest achievements. Without Concorde, there would certainly have been no Airbus. She has become iconic, a symbol of cutting edge technology, excellence and elegance. She is also a symbol of national pride—for the French, she is a French aircraft, and for the British, naturally she is a British one.

In twenty-seven years of service Concorde made more than 14,000 journeys and carried nearly 4 million passengers. Only twenty Concorde aircraft were built, six for development purposes and fourteen that undertook commercial flights. There were, in all, two prototypes, two pre-production aircraft and sixteen production models, the first two of which never operated commercially.

WHERE CAN YOU SEE THE AIRCRAFT?

THE PROTOTYPES

F-WTSS (001) was the first Concorde to fly (March 2, 1969). Since October 19, 1973, she has been on show at the Musée de l'Air et l'Espace (Air and Space Museum) at Le Bourget near Paris, having made 397 test flights, totaling more than 800 hours, including 254 at supersonic speeds.

G-BSST (002), her British counterpart, has been on display at the Fleet Air Arm Museum, Yeovilton (England) since March 4, 1976, having made 438 flights.

THE PRE-PRODUCTION AIRCRAFT

Concorde G-AXDN (101) was flown to the Imperial War Museum, Duxford (England) on August 20, 1977, after 269 flights, including 168 that broke the sound barrier. Concorde F-WTSA (102) was given to the Delta Museum, Orly (France) after 314 flights, 189 of which reached supersonic speeds.

PRODUCTION AIRCRAFT

NON-COMMERCIAL

F-WTSB (201) was donated to the Brooklands Museum at Weybridge (England), having been used by British Airways as a source of spare parts. She flew for the last time in December 1981.

AIR FRANCE'S CONCORDE AIRCRAFT

Seven Concorde airliners carried passengers in Air France's colors:

F-BTSC (203) crashed at Gonesse near Paris on July 25, 2000. She was the aircraft used in the film *Airport '79: The Concorde*.

F-BVFA (205) carries the serial number 5. Air France gave her to the National Air and Space Museum in Washington (Smithsonian Institute). This was the airplane that inaugurated Air France's first supersonic service (Paris–Dakar–Rio) on January 21, 1976. She is the oldest of Air France's Concorde fleet.

F-BVFB (207) was given to the Automobile and Technology Museum at Sinsheim as a tribute to the German victims of the disaster on July 25, 2000. She flew to Karlsruhe-Baden military airport in south-west Germany on June 24, 2003. She was partly dismantled and then taken by road and the Rhine to join a Tupulev TU-144 already on display at Sinsheim.

F-BVFC (209) returned to the Airbus factory at Toulouse-Blagnac on June 27, 2003. She will be on display at the aeronautics park, *Au Grand Toulouse, Terre d'Envol*, currently under construction. This aircraft made two round-the-world flights. The first took place from September 6–28, 1989, when she covered 51,354 km in 37 hours 25 minutes. The second was from October 10–26, 1993.

OPPOSITE
The first British Airways Concorde to enter service goes on its last journey in 2004. From Heathrow Airport it is taken by road and barge to the Scottish Museum of Flight.

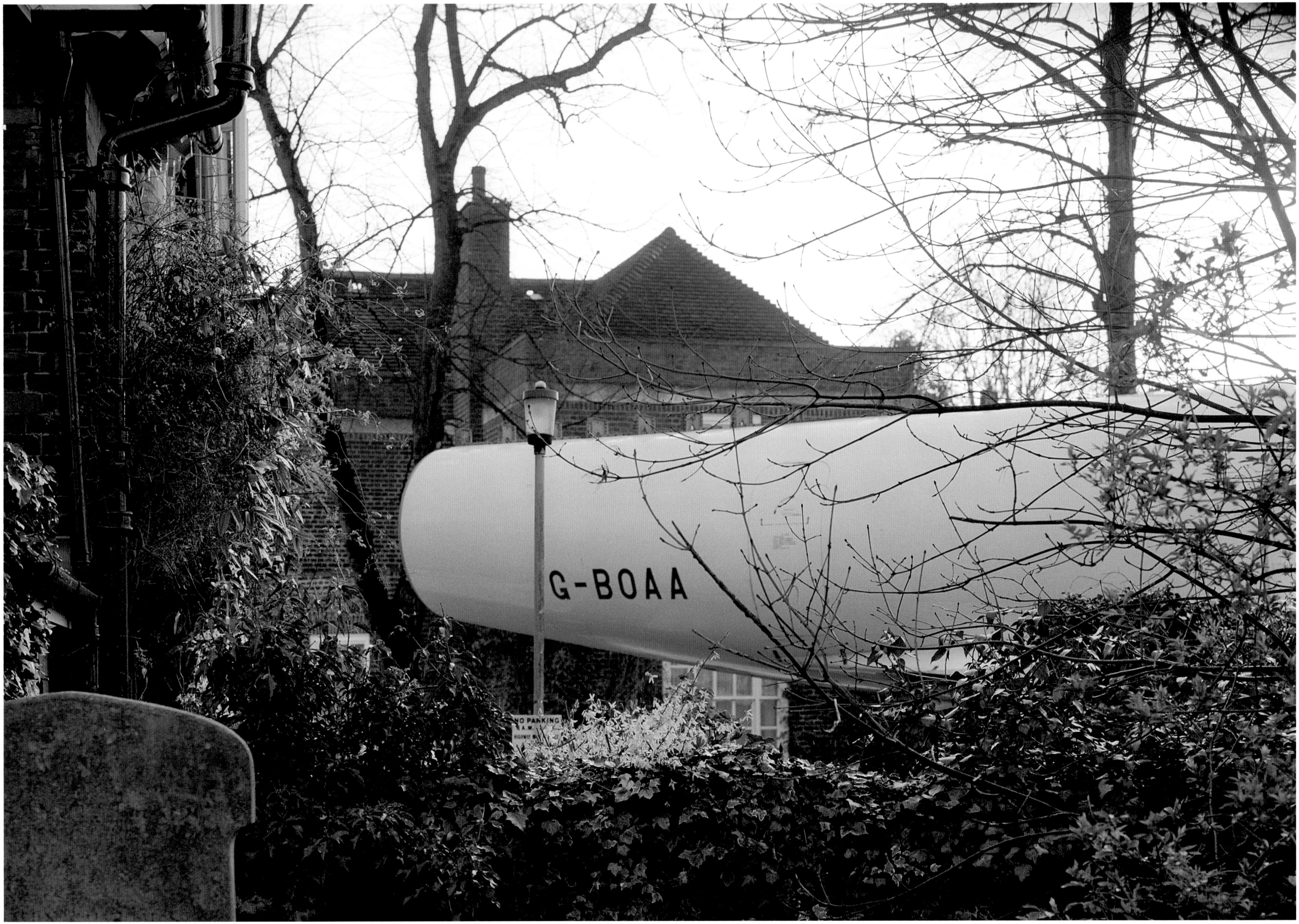
G-BOAA
NO PARKING

Concorde will never really disappear because she will never leave our imagination.

JEAN-CYRIL SPINETTA, PRESIDENT OF AIR FRANCE, APRIL 2003

F-BVFD (211) suffered a heavy landing at Dakar in November 1977, which caused airframe damage. Although she was repaired and returned to service, when the Paris-Dakar-Rio service was stopped, Air France had surplus aircraft and the F-BVFD was chosen to be retired in May 1982 after only 5,821 flying hours because of the damage previously suffered. She was then used as a source of spare parts before finally being dismantled for scrap in 1994.

F-BTSD (213) was delivered to the Air and Space Museum at Le Bourget (France) on June 14, 2003. She now stands opposite the prototype 001. This was the aircraft that took part in the vast publicity campaign on behalf of Pepsi. Sierra Delta holds the most records, including the fastest commercial flight westward round the world (33 hours in October, 1992) as well as the round-the-world record in the opposite direction, achieved three years later.

F-BVFF (215) can be found at Roissy-Charles-de-Gaulle international airport, near Air France's maintenance hangars. Her first flight was on December 26, 1978, and her last on June 14, 2000.

BRITISH AIRWAYS' CONCORDE AIRCRAFT

Seven passenger airliners also flew in the colors of British Airways:

G-BOAA (206), now on display at the Scottish National Museum of Flight, and G-BOAB (208), which can be seen at London Heathrow, both made their last round trips in August 2000 and did not fly again after the accident at Gonesse.

G-BOAC (204), the standard-bearer of the fleet because of her registration letters, BOAC (British Overseas Airlines Corporation), was taken to the Manchester Airport Aviation Viewing Park (England) on October 31, 2003.

G-BOAD (210) left Heathrow for the last time on November 10, 2003, heading for JFK Airport, New York, from where she was transferred by barge to the Intrepid Sea, Air and Space Museum, New York.

G-BOAE (212) flew for the last time to Grantley Adams Airport, Bridgetown, Barbados (West Indies) on November 17, 2003. She carried 70 British Airways executives. During her final flight, she reached the maximum certified height of 60,000 ft (18,300 m).

G-BOAF (216), the last Concorde to be built, flew for the last time on Wednesday,

November 26, 2003 when she returned to Filton, Bristol (England), where she is now on display at the Filton Visitor's Centre Airfield.

G-BOAG (214), the aircraft that made the final Speedbird 2 flight from New York on October 24, 2003, left Heathrow for the last time on November 3, 2003. She spent a day of resting and refueling in New York before, unusually, flying at supersonic speeds over the sparsely populated regions of northern Canada to Seattle, where she is on display at the Museum of Flight alongside the first-ever Boeing 747 and a BOAC Comet. This Concorde was used for spare parts before herself being restored using parts from Air France's F-BVFD.

165

OPPOSITE
Charles-de-Gaulle Airport, February 2004. Two of the most legendary aircraft in aviation history stand side by side in a hangar: Concorde F-BVFF and the DC3-BBBE.

> *We tried to make a celebration of Concorde's retirement, something that the public and the airline can remember with pride.*
>
> MIKE BANNISTER, CAPTAIN ON THE LAST BRITISH AIRWAYS COMMERCIAL FLIGHT

JUNE 24, 2003: THE FINAL FLIGHT OF F-BVFB

"The end is everything." Gérard de Nerval's words and their double meaning will be much in my mind both before and during 'FB's last flight to Germany and Baden-Baden airport (Baden Airpark). Doing justice to the event is what matters. It's the end of Concorde. It's the last flight for 'FB and, for its captain, it's the end of an all too brief career on the legendary aircraft. The end, also, of his career at Air France.

How the event is conducted is all important. To echo Nerval once more, how to live up to the importance and significance of such an event? How to add a small personal touch when, restricted by such complex technological systems and the strict criteria of their operation there is little room to make your own individual mark?

Having made the final commercial landing at Roissy-Charles-de-Gaulle the month before (a supersonic round trip on this same 'FB, chartered by Michel Thorigny and Air Loisir Services) and seeing that a huge crowd had gathered (the police had to get some cars to park on the motorway!), I knew that tens of thousands of people would converge on Baden-Baden, many of them in light aircraft and helicopters. Security was therefore, more than ever, the prime concern. I studied the flight plan with the first officer, Robert Vacchiani, and the two flight engineers, Rémi Pivet and Jean-Pierre Desserprit, and we noted that, if we did not change our approach path, we might cross into Class E airspace, running

the risk of colliding with any other aircraft there. We therefore decided to alter our path and to approach Baden-Baden directly at a height of 6,000 ft (1,829 m) and only then descend into the airfield's control zone, so avoiding potentially risky air space.

As we prepared for departure from CDG, it was clear that a big event was taking place. Many people involved with Concorde were milling around: mechanics, aircraft coordinators, crews … The mechanics initialed the shaft of the forward landing gear. Photographers were clicking away non-stop. Béatrice down below gave me one last signal … The cabin crew carried out their final preparations, among them my friend Gérard Denuit.

The aircraft was full with a hundred guests of Air France, some of whom were well-known (ambassadors, directors, former Concorde pilots, etc.) and some were Air France employees, including the mechanics who had worked with skill and passion on this exceptional aircraft for so many years. We were especially honored by having Christiane on board, widow of Captain Marty [who had died in the Gonesse crash]. This was her first and, sadly, her last flight on Concorde. We were old friends and it goes without saying that this added to the emotion of my last flight. My son Pierre-Louis was also on board for the last take-off.

We flew one last time at Mach 2 off the coast of Brittany. The weather was fine. We then turned eastwards and flew back below the

speed of sound (Mach 0.95 even so!), over landmarks such as the bay of Mont Saint-Michel and the château of Versailles. As we passed over Lorraine, French fighter planes came to pay their respects. I had given the ok to this the day before. They wisely kept their distance and we could not see them from the cockpit, but photos of 'FB, flying nose high and visor raised, were taken as a result. Unfortunately, it was cloudy on the right bank of the Rhine and we did not see the runway at Baden-Baden until we descended through the clouds directly over the airport.

This was our last opportunity to show off the aircraft. So I decided to make an extra circle by coming down the wrong way over the runway, then making a tight turn back over the airfield to fly past close to the Rhine and French airspace within sight of the runway on the right-hand side. I treated myself to an "overshoot" of the final approach, which, at least, had the advantage of showing off the aircraft turning at a steep tilt and high angle of attack. My friend, Adam Shaw, who had flown from Annecy in his Cap 10, was watching at the end of the runway with his expert eye. As we turned to make our brief final approach, we noticed there were tens of thousands of spectators.

The final landing (trouble-free, which was just as well since there was no chance of the aircraft being brought back!), the last check-list—and then it was time for the ceremony. After a media onslaught and the usual

interviews, the official handover of the aircraft took place in a nearby hangar amid an atmosphere of German jollity. Finally there were a few speeches. Mine, read in German, translated by my friend Georges Hagstotz (a 747 captain) from a text I had prepared, earned me a standing ovation.

If "to part is to die a little," I at least tried, as in the bullring, to "make a good end" in the Spanish manner.

After a brief, late visit to the museum at Sinsheim, where we all, still in uniform, climbed into the cockpit of the TU-144 for a final souvenir photo of the technical crew, there was a farewell evening in Strasbourg with the crew, then I drove home to Haute-Savoie with my wife and son.

As I drove I could not stop myself from looking in the rear-view mirror, and now, more than a year later, I still feel, and no doubt will for some time to come, a sort of dull, wistful ache.

Jean-Louis Chatelain (Commander of F-BVFB's last flight), November 2004

OPPOSITE
Concorde takes her final bow. Shortly after 17.00 on October 24, 2003, the last British Airways flight lands at London Heathrow. The airport firefighters salute her. Mike Bannister of BA's Concorde division piloted the final commercial flight.
PAGES 168, 169
LEFT & RIGHT: F-BVFD suffered a sad fate. Withdrawn from service in 1982 after a heavy landing at Dakar, Senegal, the jet airliner was used for spare parts and then cut up for scrap in 1994. Her first flight was on February 10, 1977.

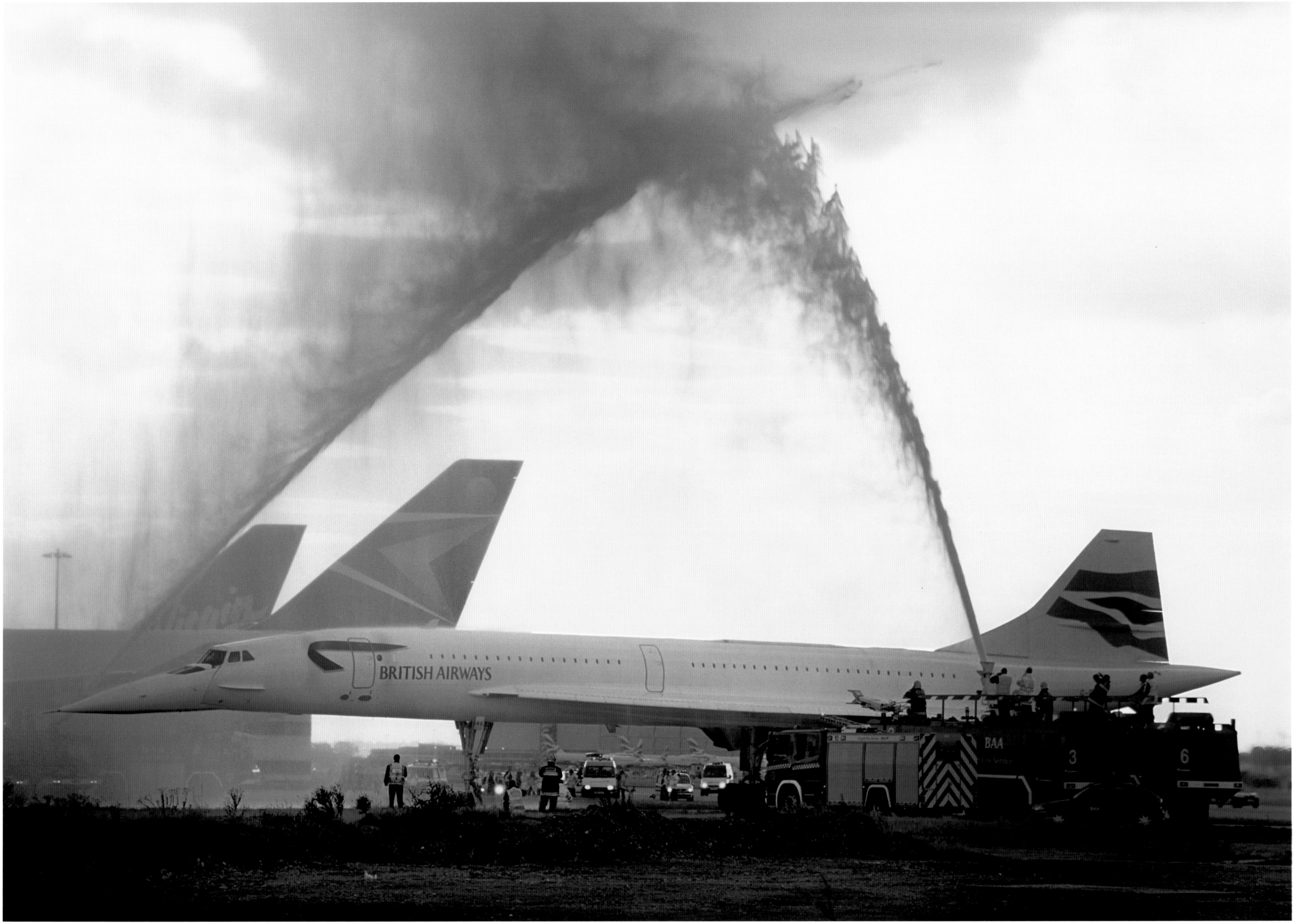
BRITISH AIRWAYS
BAA
3
6

RIGHT
Highly deceptive! In fact, the Concorde flying over this
London street is just a cardboard model.
OPPOSITE
Concorde stars in the blockbuster disaster movie, *Airport '79:
The Concorde* with Alain Delon and George Kennedy.
Unfortunately, the film was not to make such an impact
on cinema history as Concorde has done in aviation.
PAGES 170, 171
LEFT & RIGHT: Concorde became so famous that in 1979
a pinball machine manufacturer featured the aircraft in one
of their designs.

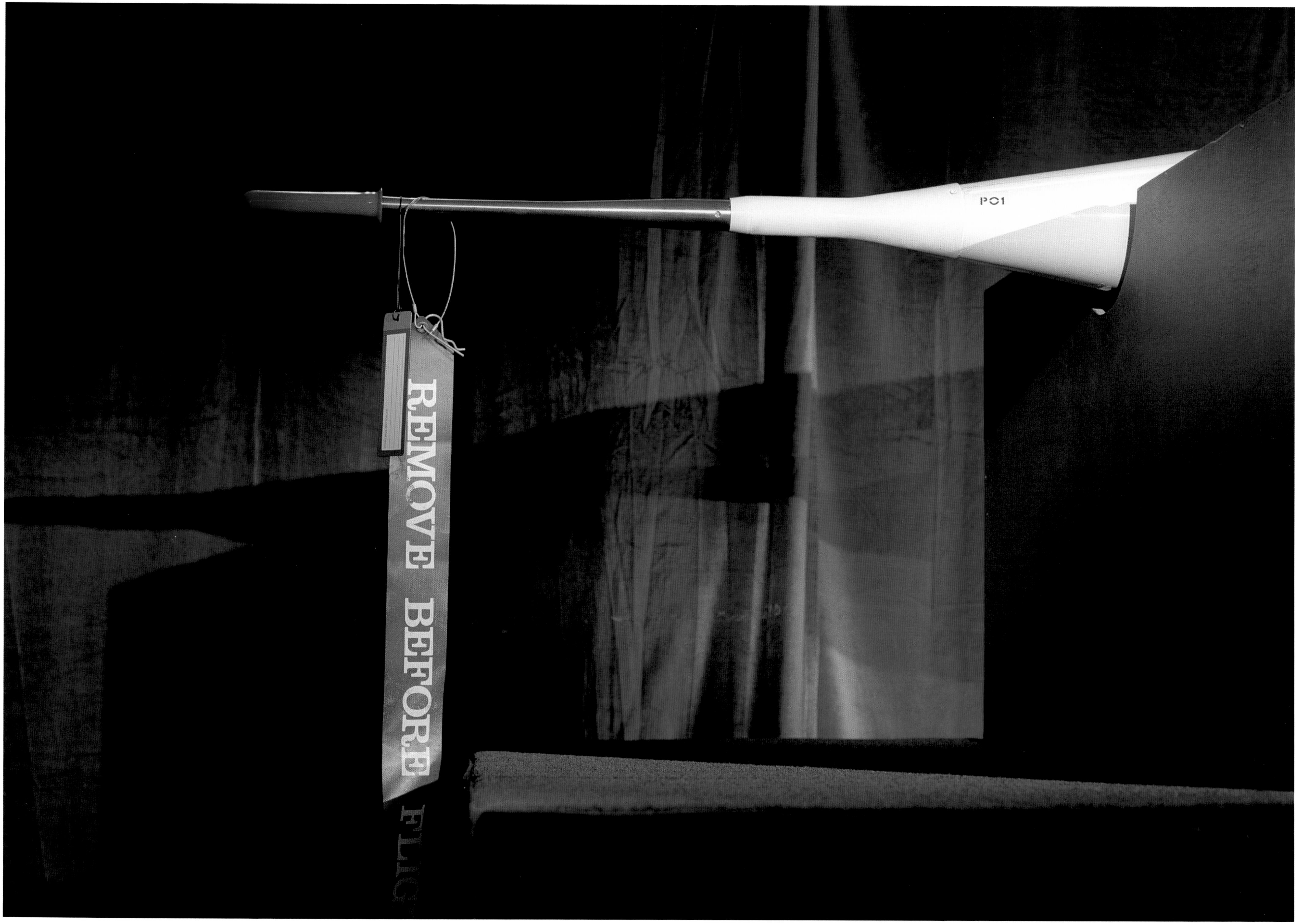
P01
REMOVE BEFORE

CONCORDE GOES UP FOR AUCTION

We absolutely must find a way to keep Concorde going.
She inspires us to keep pushing back the frontiers of our imagination.

TERENCE CONRAN, DESIGNER

A sale of Concorde memorabilia at Christie's is an exceptional event. An artificial horizon, a machmeter, an icovol (flight control indicator), a radome (nose cone), two Olympus 593 engines, a nose control—these were included in a total of around 218 lots that were difficult for the staff of the famous auction rooms to value, given the passion that Concorde arouses.

On Saturday November 15, 2003, at Christie's Paris saleroom, 9 Avenue de Matignon, the bids exceeded all expectations. The tip of Concorde's nose, the radome, was originally estimated to fetch between 10,000 and 15,000 euros ($12,000–18,000) but was sold for 420,000 euros ($500,000). One buyer treated himself to an airlock door bearing the registration name Fox Bravo for 53,000 euros ($64,500). Possibly fearing that he might be lured into buying something else, he left the room immediately the bidding was over saying, "My wife told me 'No more than 20,000 euros ($24,000)!' What's she going to say to me?" This auction, the profits from which went to the Air France foundation for children in need, raised a total of 3,295,683 euros ($4 million). But there were no affordable small lots for Concorde fans and enthusiasts of more slender means.

A few months later, British Airways organized a sale of parts at Bonham's on behalf of the charity "Get Kids Going", which encourages handicapped children to take part in sport. Interest from Concorde enthusiasts was so great that a third sale took place near Coventry on April 18, 2004. Some 150,000 Concorde parts were auctioned but this time the prices were more reasonable: even so, one Italian buyer paid 173,000 euros ($207,000 dollars) for Concorde's nose, while an Olympus engine fetched 34,690 ($41,400), and Alyson Rainer, a financial analyst working for British Airways, paid 1,206 euros ($1,440 dollars) for one of the aircraft's toilets.

OPPOSITE
The radome (protective housing for radar antenna) with its Pitot tube, which extends Concorde's slender nose. It was auctioned at Christie's for 420,000 euros ($500,000).

**Premier vol
Washington / Paris
par Concorde Air France**

AIR FRANCE
1 SQUARE MAX HYMANS
75015 PARIS

**PREMIER VOL PARIS RIO DE JANEIRO
PAR CONCORDE AIR FRANCE**

AIR FRANCE
58 AVE. PRESIDENTE
ANTONIO CARLOS
RIO DE JANEIRO

RIGHT
A special first day cover was issued to mark Concorde's first commercial flight on January 21, 1976.
OPPOSITE
More than 2,500 stamps and plate blocks (sheets of the same stamp) featuring Concorde are listed in philately catalogues. The first country to depict her on a stamp was Malaysia on August 30, 1965, when two stamps were issued showing Concorde flying over Kuala Lumpur Airport. Concorde also owes her conspicuous presence on stamps to the many stamps featuring her issued by the members of the Universal Postal Union, the organization which regulates international postal matters.

130F
3me Anniversaire du 1er Vol Commercial Supersonique
poste aérienne 1979
Frères Wright
république du MALI
L. ARQUER   EDILA

200F
3me Anniversaire du 1er Vol Commercial Supersonique
poste aérienne 1979
Lindbergh
république du MALI
L. ARQUER   EDILA

3me Anniversaire du 1er Vol Commercial Supersonique
poste aérienne 1979
Ader
paris • dakar • rio de janeiro
république du MALI
L. ARQUER   EDILA

AIR FRANCE
RÉPUBLIQUE DU NIGER   CONCORDE
Poste aérienne   300F
1983

BELIZE   E II R
WHO INTRODUCED POSTAGE STAMP CENTENARY
CONCORDE   1903-1978
th. ANNIVERSARY OF I.C.A.O.
50c

БЪЛГАРИЯ   CONCORDE   CT 25   BULGARIA
ПОЩА
Д. ТАСЕВ 1990

RÉPUBLIQUE DE CÔTE D'IVOIRE   300F
HISTOIRE DE L'AVIATION   CONCORDE

RÉPUBLIQUE DE HAUTE-VOLTA   300F
POSTE AÉRIENNE
CONCORDE

REPUBLICA DE GUINEA ECUATORIAL
5.00 EKUELE

Concorde   Rio Paris
Brasil 76   5,20
LUCIA TV RAMOS

PARAGUAY   Gs. 20.
AIR FRANCE
CONCORDE
INAUGURACIÓN DE VUELOS SUPERSÓNICOS A SUDAMÉRICA

DE LA TRAVERSÉE DE L'ATLANTIQUE PAR CHARLES LINDBERGH
50è ANNIVERSAIRE   Après 50 années, U.S.A.-France, 3 heures 55 minutes
RÉPUBLIQUE TOGOLAISE   POSTE AÉRIENNE   90F

LIBERIA 50c
SIR ROWLAND HILL 1879-1979
'FIRST POSTAGE STAMP'
CONCORDE

AIR FRANCE
1987 DPR KOREA   20

RÉPUBLIQUE DU MALI
AIR FRANCE
PHILATELIA
1973 1ere traversée directe de l'Atlantique Nord en Concorde
500F
C. JUMELET   EDILA

PRIOR

BELGIQUE-BELGIE   0,49

EUROPE AFRIQUE
RÉPUBLIQUE DE DJIBOUTI
POSTE AÉRIENNE 1981   100F
J. COMBET   EDILA

S. TOMÉ E PRÍNCIPE
1874 1878
1978
C.T.T. TOMÉ E PRÍNCIPE
15

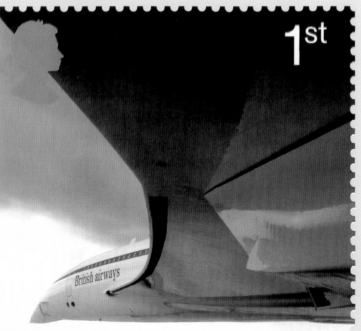

1st
British airways
1976 Concorde

4CH
BHUTAN
1874   1974
CENTENARY OF THE UNIVERSAL POSTAL UNION

LEFT
Surprisingly few posters featuring Concorde were produced.
Here is one of British Airways' posters.
OPPOSITE
A poster designed by Roger Excoffon in 1976.

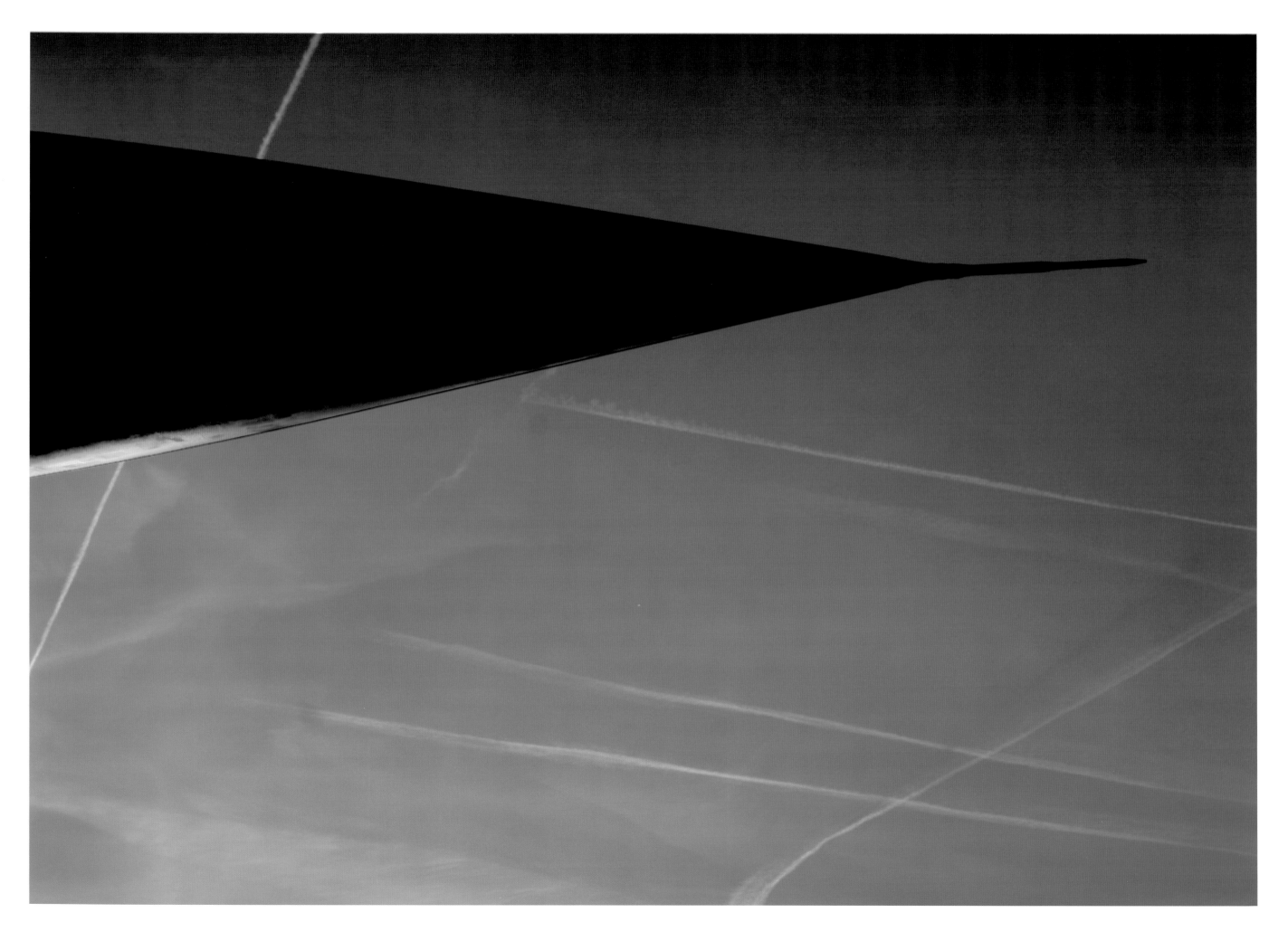

CONCORDE: SOME KEY DATES

October 25, 1962: Sud Aviation and the British Aircraft Corporation submit their plans to build a jet airliner to the French and British governments.

November 29, 1962: the Anglo-French agreement to manufacture a jet transport aircraft is signed.

January 13, 1963: Concorde acquires her name, baptized by General de Gaulle in a famous speech during which ironically he also banned Britain from entering the Common Market.

October 24, 1963: the first life-sized model of Concord (without the "e") is put on display in Bristol. A controversy about the aircraft's name ensues.

November 19, 1964: following the British general election, the new Labour government announces that Britain is withdrawing from the project, but reverses this decision two months later.

April 7, 1966: the final assembly of the prototype "Concorde 001" gets underway at Toulouse.

December 11, 1967: the first French prototype, F-WTSS, leaves the hangars at Toulouse.

September 19, 1968: the first British prototype, G-BSST, "rolls out", i.e. leaves the hangars at Filton, Bristol.

March 2, 1969: the first flight by F-WTSS with André Turcat at the controls (duration: 29 minutes).

April 9, 1969: the first flight of G-BSST, piloted by Brian Trubshaw.

October 1, 1969: Concorde 001 breaks the sound barrier during its forty-fifth test flight.

November 4, 1970: Concorde 001 goes through Mach 2.

November 12, 1970: Concorde 002 also goes through Mach 2.

May 25, 1971: Concorde 001 makes the first intercontinental test flight, between Paris and Dakar.

April 28, 1972: BOAC places its first order for five aircraft.

October 9, 1975: Concorde receives its French airworthiness certificate.

December 5, 1975: Concorde receives its British airworthiness certificate.

January 21, 1976: the first commercial flights. Two Concordes took off simultaneously (co-ordinated by radio contact). One (Air France) left Paris for Rio de Janeiro via Dakar, the other (British Airways) left London for Bahrain.

April 9, 1976: opening of the Paris–Caracas service with a stopover at Santa Maria.

May 24, 1976: the special flight of two Concordes between Paris, London and Washington, DC, with a parallel fly-past and landing at Washington-Dulles airport.

November 23, 1977: the launch of the regular service between Paris and New York.

April 1, 1982: the closure of the services to Rio de Janeiro and Caracas.

May 2, 1989: Pope John Paul II travels from Reunion to Lusaka (Zambia) on board Concorde F-BTSC.

October 12, 1992: an Air France Concorde flies east-to-west around the world in 33 hours 27 minutes, beating the record for a commercial aircraft.

July 25, 2000: a Concorde with 113 people aboard crashes at Gonesse near Roissy-Charles-de-Gaulle.

August 10, 2000: Air France suspends supersonic flights.

August 15, 2000: British Airways follows suit. The next day the aircraft's certificate of airworthiness is withdrawn.

September 5, 2001: Concorde regains her certificate of airworthiness after undergoing numerous modifications.

November 7, 2001: the resumption of commercial flights from Paris and London to New York.

May 31, 2003 at 17.45: Concorde's last commercial flight in Air France livery ends.

October 24, 2003: Concorde's last commercial flight in British Airways livery.

PHOTOGRAPHIC CREDITS

© Aerospace Imaging/PPL: 114

© Aérospatiale/Airbus aérothèque: 55, 62–63, 64, 65, 66-67, 111, 124–125, 153

© Airbus: 30-31, 32, 35, 38, 39, 40, 41, 48–49, 50, 56, 57, 60

© British Airways Plc http://www.bamuseum.com: 68, 76, 80, 96, 106, 107, 112, 161, 172

© Gabriel Cabos: 168, 169

© Éric Celerier: 86

© Bernard Charles: 158–159, 167

© Collection Bernard Charles—AIACC Club Concorde: 176, 177

© Collection Jean Dieuzaide: 157

© Collection Musée Air France: 6–7, 20–21, 103, 104, 105, 113, 115, 119, 126 (photo by Remy Poinot), 132, 133, 139, 140, 141, 146, 148, 149, 178 (poster by Roger Excoffon)

© Private collection: 116–117

© Crowell/Reuters-Max PPP: 98

© François Delebecque: 109, 110

© Laurent Desmarest: 12–13

© Jean Dieuzaide: 24–25, 26, 27, 33, 43, 47, 52–53, 58–59, 69, 78, 79, 121, 127

© D.R. (design: Terence Conran): 108

© ECPAD France: 28

© Michel Fraile: 2, 150, 152, 154–155 (poster by Raymond Moretti), 164, 170, 171, 180

© History Office, Edwards AFB: 16–17, 18

© Keystone: 74, 75

© Magnum Photos/Raymond Depardon: 85

© Magnum Photos/Erich Hartmann: 51

© Magnum Photos/Peter Marlow: 10, 122, 123, 160, 163, 174

© Jean Nakashima: 130–131

© Philippe Noret: 3, 147

© ONERA: 36

© Eduardo Pocaï: 83

© John Powell: 70

© Benoît Rajau: 134–135, 136–137, 142, 143, 144, 145, 151

© Jonathan Safford: 87, 100–101

© SNECMA: 45

© Universal Films: 173

© E.J. Van Koenigsveld: 94, 95

© M. Wagner/Aviation-images.com: 4, 8-9, 72–73, 88, 90-91, 92, 128–129

ACKNOWLEDGMENTS

No one can be indifferent to Concorde. Everyone who has been connected with her, however closely or otherwise, has moving memories of her. It is both thanks to them and for them that this book has been written.

The authors would like to thank
In particular Jacqueline Dieuzaide, enthusiastic and passionate promoter of the work of Jean Dieuzaide, one of the great photographers of the twentieth century, and also Denis Parenteau, president of the Air France Museum.

For their help, enthusiastic involvement and friendly collaboration:
Jacques Arnould, Olivier Beaudon, Luc Berger of Dassault Aviation, Caroline Cadier, Pierrette Cathala, Eric Celerier, Guy Cervelle, Bernard Charles, Jean-Louis Chatelain, Edouard Chemel, Edgard Chillaud, Gérard David, director of communication at Dassault, Franck Debouck, Elisabeth Fedith of ONERA, Daniel Frigo, Gérard Gabrilot, Alain Grassi of SNECMA, Aline Henry, Anne-Marie Hudv of Christie's, Paris, Paul Jarvis and all the team at the British Airways Museum, Raymond Machavoine, Aline Magne, Pascale Montmarson, Sonia Ountzian,

Robert Peltrie of the Historical Department of British Airways, Alain Piccinini, Alain Postigo of Airbus Industries, Hubert Protin, Christine Scazza, Philippe-Michel Thibaud, André Turcat, Béatrice Vialle, all employees of Air France and British Airways in London and Paris.

For their valuable personal accounts:
Patrick Baudry, François de Closet, Terence Conran, Gérard Depardieu, Raymond Depardon, Alain Ducasse, Philippe Faure-Brac, Yannick Noah, Andrée Putman, Mstislav Rostropovitch.

For their splendid pictures:
All the photographers, well-known and less well-known, who have spent so many hours "hunting down" Concorde: Gabriel Cabos, François Delebecque, Laurent Desmaret, Raymond Depardon, Jean Dieuzaide, Eric Domage, Anthony J. Best, Christoph Lachmund, Jin Nakashima, Philippe Noret, Eduardo Pocaï, John Powell, Benoît Rajau, Bill Ramsey, Jonathan Safford, Peter Unmuth, E.J. Van Konigsveld.

As well as…
Patrick Bordenave, Pierre Bourgin, Christian Brincourt, Jean-Claude Chobert, Gabriel Evesque, Gérard Feldzer, Françoise Payen, Lucio Perinotto, Emmanuelle Perrier, Michel Polacco, Véronique Reynier, Mathew Riches, Corinne Tourne, Pierre Sparaco, Victoria Yeager.

And finally…
Frédéric Beniada thanks Charlotte for her patience and Michel Fraile thanks Juliette for her friendly interest.

To all those who have been forgotten, the authors request that they accept their sincere apologies.

The editor would like to thank:
Michel Fraile, for having put so much energy, enthusiasm, time and passion into the making of this book.

Warm thanks also to Christelle Chevallier, Andrea Field, Natalie Lefèbvre and Laurent Nicole.

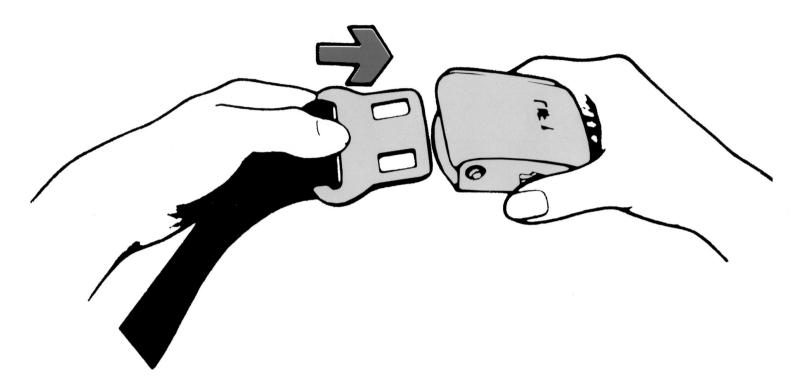

Editor
Odile Perrard

Art Editor
Sabine Houplain

Design and layout
Rachel Cazadamont of H5

Production
Felicity O'Connoer

Reproduction
Sele Offset

Printed in Malaysia by
Tien Wah Press

English translation by
JMS Books LLP

This edition first published in 2006 by Zenith
Press, an imprint of MBI Publishing Company,
Galtier Plaza, Suite 200, 380 Jackson Street,
St. Paul, MN 55101-3885 USA

Copyright © 2005 by
Editions EpA/Hachette-Livre

English language translation copyright
© 2006 by Editions EpA/Hachette-Livre

All rights reserved. With the exception of
quoting brief passages for the purposes of
review, no part of this publication may be
reproduced without prior written permission
from the Publisher.

The information in this book is true and
complete to the best of our knowledge. All
recommendations are made without any
guarantee on the part of the author or
Publisher, who also disclaim any liability
incurred in connection with the use of this data
or specific details.

This publication has not been prepared,
approved, or licensed by Aerospatiale,
British Aircraft Corporation, or their
successors.

We recognize, further, that some words,
model names, and designations mentioned
herein are the property of the trademark
holder. We use them for identification purposes
only. This is not an official publication.

MBI Publishing Company titles are also
available at discounts in bulk quantity for
industrial or sales-promotional use.
For details write to Special Sales Manager at
MBI Publishing Company, Galtier Plaza,
Suite 200, 380 Jackson Street, St. Paul, MN
55101-3885 USA

ISBN-13: 978-0-7603-2703-6
ISBN-10: 0-7603-2703-3